Raphael's Treatment Protocol

Author

Barry Hardy

Raphael's Treatment Protocol

Copyright © 2009 Barry Hardy publications which is part of BH Management Services Ltd, London UK

The pre launch version of this book was published 06th February 2009 in Great Britain with First Edition published 20th March 2009.

All rights reserved. No part of this book may be reproduced or transmitted in any form or by any means without written permission of the author.

ISBN 978-0-9561538-0-7

Discover more at www.barryhardy.com

My body is the greatest healer of them all and my mind is its engine

DECENCY WARNING

Please note that Raphael's Treatment Protocol contains strong, explicit views including the use of offensive language, which some may find unnecessarily gratuitous. Therefore please don't read this book if you are easily offended by:

- Strong views.
- Strong language.
- Grammatical inconsistencies.

Or

- Personal experiences and perceptions expressed freely.

DEDICATION

This book is dedicated to the battalions of helpless souls butchered in the killing fields of medical man. We who survive will do our level best to right their wrongs. *Note Raphael's Treatment Protocol was written and complied entirely in a multicultural internet café in south London and I thank my hosts profoundly for their unequivocal generosity and continued support of my endeavours on this front.*

My body is the greatest healer of them all and my mind is its engine

DISCLAIMER

The information provided in this book should not be construed as personal medical or clinical advice or instruction no action should be taken based solely on the contents of this book. Readers should consult appropriate professionals on any matter relating to their health and well being. The information and opinions provided here are for personal research purposes only. Readers who fail to consult appropriate professionals assume the risk of incurring injury and must accept any consequences directly or indirectly associated with their personal actions on any and all related matters.

I now know; who I am, what I am and what I can do, for I am now pain free

FOREWORD

This book will postulate alternative slants on aspects of chronic illness, hence opening up new ways of thought, new ways of seeing and new ways of dealing with chronic illness expression. Because once we appreciate the entire picture that generates chronic illness, its effective diagnosis and treatment options, then we have the power to take control of it and our lives once again. I believe that we all have the right to be all that we were ever born to be. But to achieve that upon a background of chronic ill health we need to let go of and free ourselves from ignorant medical prejudices the serve only to hold us back. So that we the former sufferers of chronic illness can soar once more in our own unique skies and in doing so, leave the pain of our chronic illness far behind us. Sure in the knowledge that chronic illness expression can never again rule any aspect of our mortality, save for sharing our knowledge of recovering from it, with those amongst us who are willing and capable of learning the gifts and messages that we have to offer. I have no medical or clinical qualifications and so none of my books prescribe anything other than the formula that I was forced to develop to aid my own unique recovery from chronic and unrelenting ill health.

My body is the greatest healer of them all and my mind is its engine

SEARCHING FOR THE TRUTH

No living man knows what mortality in all its normality truly is, until he has been either forced to endure and/or blessed to survive the absurdity and sheer intolerability of apparently irresolvable chronic ill health. For that is a place where no fellow man hears any heartfelt and/or desperate pleas for help, because in that place and in that space there is not one ounce or shred of humanistic decency. It is a place where your body apparently delights in tormenting your very existence and a place where medics with sickening guile, spew their ignorant dogma to you and about you but offer absolutely no help, support or hope for the entirety of your passage through that place. Such is the depravity of that place and space that; release from mortality becomes an overriding preoccupation for anyone unfortunate enough to find themselves trapped within the same. It is a place where the light refuses to shine with endless penchant, for it is eclipsed almost continually by the purgatory of mortality in and of simply monumental proportions. So let's be very clear here, let no man in your presence ever attempt to liken this place and space with the simplicity of any given minor mortal imposition. For true mortal suffering under whatever presentation it chooses to manifest itself, is not a club or requiring of any arm bands of unity or honour. Because it is a place and time in your mortal passage that is as depraved and dark as mortal suffering can be.

I now know; who I am, what I am and what I can do, for I am now pain free

All that being said; I believe that mortal suffering is an unacceptable blight upon the reality of mortality which we must do our level best to eradicate from society if we do nothing else over the next 100 years. Because whilst it may well be a natural dynamic of normal mortality. Simply accepting mortal suffering in any way shape or form because it makes the lives of others much easier is both ethically and morally reprehensible. My personal experiences at the hands of the medical industry continue to generate grave reservations in me about the integrity, decency, credibility and morality of those engaged in medicine and that's why I implore kindred souls to take great care when interacting with the same. You see; only those who have suffered at the hands of the medical industry and yet somehow also managed to survive their so called care' are able to personally validate just how despicably poor, unsupportive and divisive that industry truly is. It is an industry rotten to the core and lacking collaterally in any tangible intellect, integrity and decency across the board and that's why I was forced to explore my own mortality and therein document my chronic ill health resolution in my books. Because whilst I cannot right any wrongs committed to me by my fellow man. The truth of the matter is that as a mortal living amongst mortals' social intercourse with our medical industry is almost certainly heading our way in any one of a hundred forms in the not too distant future and that I'm afraid to say is fact.

My body is the greatest healer of them all and my mind is its engine

Nevertheless the questions I believe that you the reader will be better able to ask yourself once you've read this book are; do I believe what any medic is saying to me now and/or in the future and more importantly; have I ever been told the truth at any point in my life by a medic? You see; truths present themselves in many differing forms i.e. the intellectualized truth, the dogmatic truth, the cultural truth and/or the politically motivated truth. However it's not until we've either tested the validity and/or experienced the stupidity of any given truth that we're in the best possible position to judge and hence re-evaluate the truth of any given truth that we've previously allowed ourselves to believe. Because of that you may even read this book and think blimey this guy is a complete waste of space and off his head or indeed you may even think; 'hmnnnn some of this makes sense, and because of that I'm willing to explore my own perceptions.

Either way;

It doesn't really make any difference to me what you think about me, about my ideas and/or my postulations for wellbeing in the greater scheme of things. Because all that should be important to you as a chronic illness sufferer is how best you can improve upon your current quality of life. All I will ever say in my own personal defense is that unlike some of the procrastinating numpties (*self obsessed theorizing so called experts and/or self appointed experts*) that we all have the potential to meet along the way from the medical industry. I've actually walked my talk and healed myself, whilst other so called enlightened experts simply sat back and wrote me off.

I now know; who I am, what I am and what I can do, for I am now pain free

So that now and after one hellish struggle for better health, it is my considered belief that chronic illness is nothing more than an expression of disease and therefore does not originate from insanity or emotional instability. Accept that and you're at least part of the way to understanding that; the originators of chronic illness are always;

    a. Physical diseases and/or rarely injury to the brain.

Or

    b. Bodily process failure and/or deviations from normal functioning.

Or

    c. Inflammation generated through diseases or injury.

Or

    d. Toxic body syndrome generated through, physical disease, bodily process failure and/or deviations from normal functioning and Inflammation generated through diseases or injury.

So then; if you're currently suffering from any form of chronic illness and/or have suffered from a chronic illness condition in the past and wish to unravel the truth about everything associated with that expression of disease, then perhaps you should;

- Stay open and consider fully any and all of my postulations for the pursuit of well-being that I explore, before deciding upon the most appropriate approach or course of action for you.

And

- Always work with or at least consult with; a suitably qualified service provider before making changes to any or all of your current treatment protocols.

But

- Under NO circumstance must you STOP taking or STOP participating in any treatment protocol designed to support your wellbeing in the absence of suitable qualified service provider because to do so would be foolish and irresponsible and you could put your long term wellbeing at significant risk.

ACKNOWLEDGMENTS

My sincere thanks go out to:

My lovely Karina without who's love and support for and of me there would have been no mortal redemption or hope for me.

Dr Sarah Myhill and Hania Baker for all their support and generosity towards my wellbeing and clinical care.

Mrs Edna Garrick for her generosity in agreeing to proof read my manuscript for me.

Mr Abdi Nur Ali, Mr. Dahir Nur Ali and Mr Abdikarin Mohamed for their generosity during the compilation of this book in their internet café on Westow Hill.

Finally to all the medical and clinical incompetents that I've encountered thus far, you are the only reason for this books production. I always knew that there was an answer to my problem and having proved that I'm now happy to share it with the world.

My body is the greatest healer of them all and my mind is its engine

ESSENTIAL READING

Everything covered in this book draws upon my own detailed personal passage through chronic illness that I cover in my book *Raphael's Legacy*. To ensure that you understand and / or do not either misinterpret or misrepresent any statement, phrase or passage in this book, please ensure that you have read Raphael's Legacy prior to exploring the subtle nuances of this book. It is also important to note that I have covered specific illnesses in a series of books which are derivatives of Raphael's Legacy. Therefore I would respectfully suggest that if you have a specific chronic illness which is either directly or indirectly causing you some degree of distress and / or driving your interest in reading this book. If you haven't read Raphael's Legacy then you must explore that first or at the very least the most relevant single illness books in relation to your chronic illness prior to exploring this book. In that way you can ensure that you fully understand why I say the things I say and why I propose the things in the way that I propose them in this book. For your reference a listing of all those support books is at your disposal on the next page. Finally and above all things, please ensure that as you move towards better health always ensure that you are adequately supported by a suitably qualified professional service provider.

I now know; who I am, what I am and what I can do, for I am now pain free

Further personal insight and self help books written by Barry Hardy in relation to Raphael's Legacy and Raphael's Treatment Protocol include:

- Stress at Close Quarters
- Anxiety at Close Quarters
- Exploring Fluid Normality
- Arthritis at Close Quarters
- Depression at Close Quarters
- Fibromyalgia at Close Quarters
- Lymes Disease at Close Quarters
- Gulf War Syndrome at Close Quarters
- Toxic Body Syndrome at Close Quarters
- Myalgic Encephalopathy at Close Quarters
- Chronic Fatigue Syndrome at Close Quarters
- Bipolar / Manic Depression at Close Quarters
- Obsessive Compulsive Disorder at Close Quarters

You can purchase any of these books at www.barryhardy.com

My body is the greatest healer of them all and my mind is its engine

CONTENTS

Decency warning 3
Dedication 4
Disclaimer 5
Foreword 6
Searching for the truth 7
Acknowledgments 12
Essential reading 13
Contents 15
Raphael's treatment protocol structure 17
Exploring the journey into darkness pragmatically 19
Exploring the darker side of medicine pragmatically 31
Exploring psychological illness pragmatically 41
Exploring personal mind anger pragmatically 57
Exploring treatment options pragmatically 65
Exploring the insanity of testing pragmatically 129
Exploring analytical testing options pragmatically 153

I now know; who I am, what I am and what I can do, for I am now pain free

Exploring raphael's treatment protocol pragmatically 159
Authors notes 189
Web sites you may wish to explore 195
Other books by barry hardy 196
Decency Warning.. 197

My body is the greatest healer of them all and my mind is its engine

RAPHAEL'S TREATMENT PROTOCOL STRUCTURE

This book consists of eight key sections, where I sequentially;

1. Explore my decline into chronic ill health because that decline and that personal process of despair and enlightenment that I was forced to go through underwrites the very idea and reasons for change in our collective perceptions and attitudes towards the effect diagnosis and treatment of chronic illness.

2. Explore the darker side of medicine during my decline into chronic ill health in doing so proactively advocating the reason for change in our collective perceptions and attitudes towards that industry from both sufferers and practitioners alike.

3. Explore the myth that our psychology is the generator and/or originator of all chronic illness states and in doing so proactively advocating the reason for change in our collective perceptions and attitudes towards that industry from both sufferers and practitioners alike.

I now know; who I am, what I am and what I can do, for I am now pain free

4. Explore mind anger resulting from failures of due diligence and care from the medical industry during my chronic illness both excusing it and citing it as possibly essential parts of our overall healing process.

5. Exploring the myriad of treatment protocols that I had undertook in pursuit of wellness, in doing so proactively advocating the reason for change in our collective perceptions and attitudes towards treatment options from both sufferers and practitioners alike.

6. Exploring the insanity that can be diagnostic analysis, in doing so proactively advocating the reason for change in our collective perceptions and attitudes towards diagnostic testing from both sufferers and practitioners alike.

7. Exploring testing options that proved beneficial to myself, in doing so proactively advocating the reason for change in our collective perceptions and attitudes towards determining root cause analysis via effective and focused analytical testing from both sufferers and practitioners alike.

8. Exploring the key steps required to support wellness via, testing, root cause analysis, control agents determination, cellular cleansing requirements and summary cost analysis that I myself developed and undertook in my pursuit of my owe pursuit of wellness.

My body is the greatest healer of them all and my mind is its engine

EXPLORING THE JOURNEY INTO DARKNESS PRAGMATICALLY

Exploration One

I now know; who I am, what I am and what I can do, for I am now pain free

Raphael's Treatment Protocol

My body is the greatest healer of them all and my mind is its engine

My decline into chronic ill health and intense chronic illness expression resulted from over three decades of medical/clinical abuse and neglect and you can read more about that in my book *Raphael's Legacy*. Nevertheless as a guy who's been through a horrific state of undiagnosed disease I realise now that the fall from good health into that of a chronic diseased state is not always a straight forward process and can take many years. The thing is we have nothing without good health, no prosperity, no career or joy, yet good health is something we all take for granted until it's ripped forever from our grasp. As a society we're not programmed to explore and look for answers when our health is in decline, because we absolve ourselves of that responsibility and empower only a select few. Therein we lose the connection that we need to plot and determine the origin and cause of our disease because as our body's sole custodian we ultimately hold all the answers and that is the only true key to recovery. As part of the foundation work required to support my diseased state postulation it was important for me in the preparation of my book *Raphael's Legacy* that I mapped and shared with you my own personal health decline, for in that process all the connections are clearly defined. With a simple red line mapping depression expression, a blue line mapping physical strength and green line mapping my emotional strength over an entire forty year period.

I now know; who I am, what I am and what I can do, for I am now pain free

Raphael's Treatment Protocol

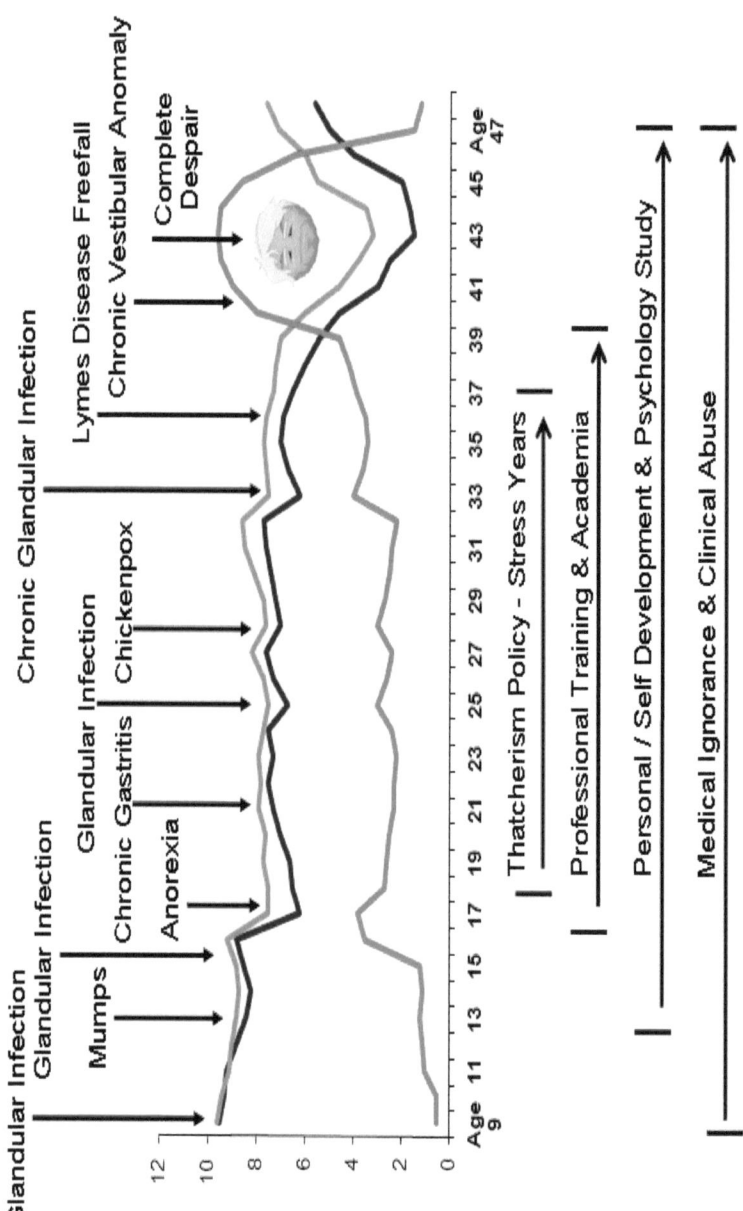

My body is the greatest healer of them all and my mind is its engine

Before I elaborate further upon my own health decline however it's important that I cover emotional and depressive state perceptions because they are frequently cited by medical charlatans as the originators of illness. When in reality they are nothing more than an expression of disease. Nevertheless there is a big difference between emotional state and depressive state and they must never be confused or directly linked as one in the same because they are not, *but I will qualify this point further in subsequent chapters.* Our emotional state in essence is our ability to cope, to rise to a challenge, to pick ourselves up after a set back and/or to project ourselves into the future and is nothing more than a derivative of our endocrine functionality.

Whereas depression I'm prepared to argue is nothing more than a symptom of disease and should not therefore be confused with subtle mood swings which are part of our normal emotional expressions. As you will observe my health profile map starts way back at the point of formalized body awareness for me where I'm aware that I had exceptionally high levels of physical endurance and emotional strength with low depression intent i.e. I simply coped, laughed and joked. Those expressions are mapped such that, physical and emotional scores at ten indicate high energy levels and equally very strong emotional stability. Whereas zero would indicate that I have no energy, no resilience, no emotional rigidity, no fight, in essence I'm simply burnt out. In terms of depression expression, zero on the map indicates no depression present whereas ten would indicate chronic suicidal depression. As my health declined it's easy to see the correlation between physical strength and emotional strength and the impact that disease has upon all three states i.e. physical and emotional states decline in vitality and depression increases with paradoxical ferocity during chronic disease. Therefore my primary postulation is that the vast majority of depressive states are a direct result

I now know; who I am, what I am and what I can do, for I am now pain free

of a diseased state and that depression is not the generator of illness as most medics would have us believe. Depression in itself is not an illness in the vast majority of cases; rather it is merely a symptom that simply manifests through disease. Equally; psychological stress is not the originator of fatigue at best it is merely a bit player or derivative of the same diseased state. It is therefore very important that we all understand that the originator of chronic symptomology is not the fault of the patient it is nothing more than an indicator of disease. Understand that and you're at least part of the way to accepting that you have a condition in Chronic illness which needs treating and that you're not the entire cause of all your presenting symptoms.

In the absence of medical/clinical scientific intellect, my battle for resolution from chronic illness expression took me to places where I would hope no fellow mortal should ever have to go. It cost me my career, my prosperity, my homes and ultimately could have cost me my life had I not been blessed with a little bit of luck and a body and mind that refused to be written off. After three decades of suffering and at a cost of over 300k I was diagnosed with Lyme's Disease, but that process despite all the self sacrifice it required on a physical, emotional, spiritual and financial level, gave birth to a man who now knows:

1. The truth about our medical/clinical industry, all it's failing, ignorance and lack of scientific validity!

And

2. What is needed on the part of any mortal to get well from a whole host of hitherto so called untreatable and/or so called psychological conditions!

My body is the greatest healer of them all and my mind is its engine

Raphael's Treatment Protocol

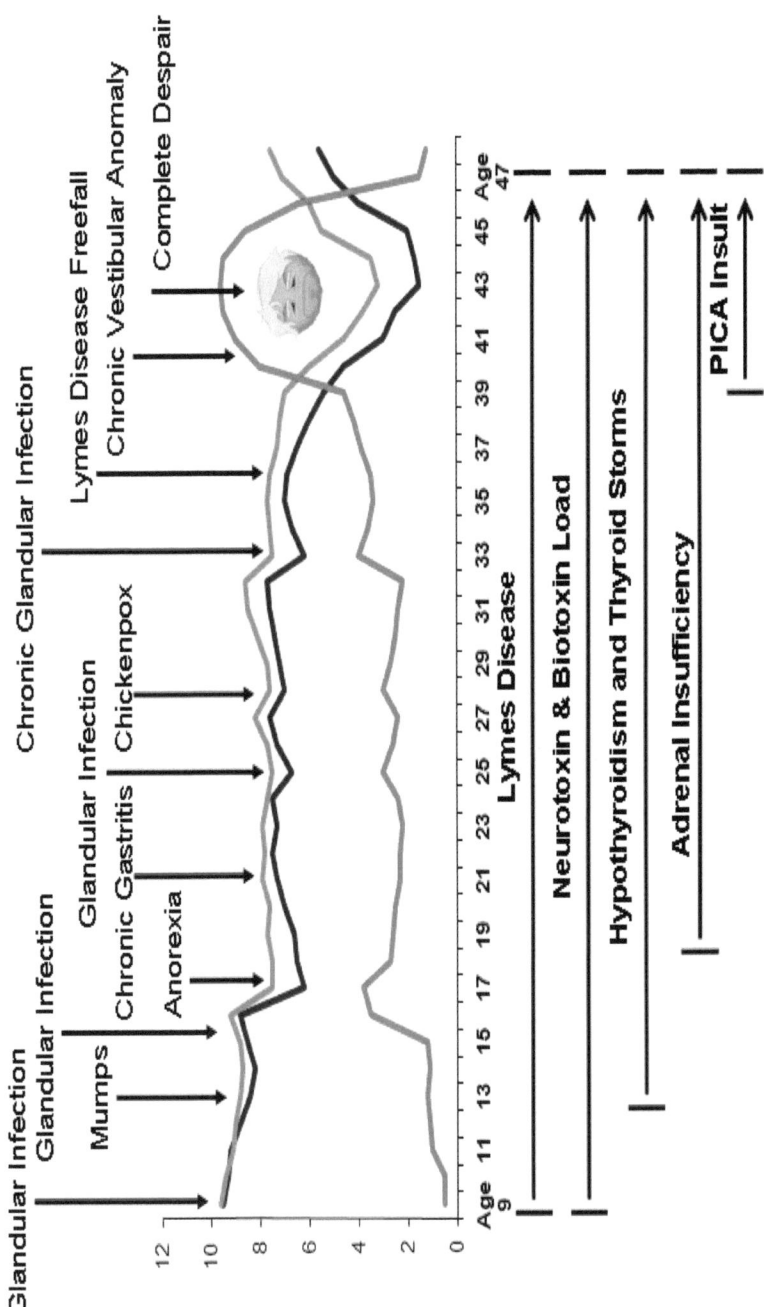

I now know; who I am, what I am and what I can do, for I am now pain free

In pursuit of my own personal well being I discovered that:

- I contacted Lymes Disease at a very young age the impact of which was that it compromised my liver, my brain and my endocrine system re: *Raphael's Legacy*

- My bodily systems were simply unable to cope with that untreated load and so over the years battling to solve my body's infection, my body simply burnt itself out, re: *Raphael's Legacy*

- When exposed to even higher levels of Lymes Disease my limited defenses were simply overrun and my health simply went into freefall and I moved very quickly into a rampant Lymes Diseased state and toxic body syndrome, re: *Raphael's Legacy*

- A situation compounded still further by the chronic activation of a simply horrendous vascular vestibular insult which was completely poo poo'd by the medical / clinical charlatans that I saw until I was able to prove its origin via self-funded imaging and neurosurgery re: *Raphael's Legacy*.

My body is the greatest healer of them all and my mind is its engine

Now the question is;

Are you open enough, ready enough and / or willing enough to explore your own chronic illness from a whole new perspective in an attempt to move both it and you into a new holistic place of considered and greater understanding?

If so;

Then take a deep breath and prepare for a bumpy yet hopefully rewarding ride, because some of the material I'm going to cover from now on in this book may simply shock you to your core.

But hey:

That's okay and I'm sure you'll agree otherwise you wouldn't be reading this book right now would you?

What you may ask has all this got to do with chronic illness? Well the answer is, not one single medic or clinician helped me when I was being destroyed by a horrendous disease despite that fact that my chronic illness levels were as chronic as it's possible to be. All they ever did was write me off at worst and at best offer me, medications that offered no resolution or hope for me. The plain disagreeable fact of the matter is that there are no medics or clinicians out there who remotely understand disease or chronic illness which means that we're completely devoid of help at the point our body moves into a chronic diseased state. What's even worse is that by the time our bodies decline into a chronic diseased state the root cause of our disease on our records is so hidden or masked by psychological inaccuracies or simply medical clap trap that the possibility of securing an effective diagnosis is in reality highly remote. I know of far too many people myself included who've been tortured by disease and ultimately chronic illness expression who've been ignored and abused wholesale by the medical/clinical world through dogma, ignorance and incompetence in terms of trying to find a scientific solution to our disease state conditions, to such an extent that it's an absolute bloody scandal. A situation which directly forced me to explore why it was that the medical/clinical world was so reluctant to help people in despair and what needed to change to bring about greater receptivity.

My body is the greatest healer of them all and my mind is its engine

During my endeavours on this matter I found only to my great annoyance that the medical/clinical industries including everyone who either works in it or supports it are simply:

- Happy with underperformance and shoddy service delivery.

- Happy to continually write its customer base off whilst continuously seeking to self elevate its/their own status through bullshit and medical/clinical ignorance and dogma.

It is an industry;

- So locked in inertia that its own scientific base is at least one hundred years ahead of its own front end service provision.

Now I'm in no way saying that in order to recover from chronic illness we all must plot our decline in health similar to the detail that I myself was forced to do so, to enable me to pass though my horrendous and deep black hole. But what I am saying is that there is a need for a significant change in our perceptions about the way we currently perceive poor health and in particular chronic illness because without that; there is very little potential for symptom free resolution and long term recovery. Therefore the key to freedom from self destruct or medical/clinical abuse in terms of chronic illness expression is to always remember that chronic illness; no matter what form it takes is always the result of anyone or all of the following:

1. Physical diseases.
2. Rarely injury to the brain.
3. Bodily process failure and/or deviations from normal functioning.
4. Inflammation generated through diseases.
5. Inflammation generated through injury to the brain.
6. Toxic body syndrome generated through, physical disease, bodily process failure and/or deviations from normal functioning and inflammation generated through diseases or injury.

My body is the greatest healer of them all and my mind is its engine

EXPLORING THE DARKER SIDE OF MEDICINE PRAGMATICALLY

Exploration Two

I now know; who I am, what I am and what I can do, for I am now pain free

My body is the greatest healer of them all and my mind is its engine

You may be surprised to read this, but let me send a shock wave racing right through your body because I'm going to empower you with a very distasteful truth. You see, at the point you move into a state of chronic ill health and/or chronic illness the deadliest people you will ever meet are those who work within and/or who support the medical/clinical world.

So much so that I'm somewhat embarrassed these days by the fact that whilst many turned their back during the greedy and wasted Thatcher and Major years. I spent a great deal of my youth campaigning and lobbying against local and central government with passion on a whole host of issues, not least to save what I felt was a laudable institution under threat, namely our glorious NHS. 'Boy did I get it wrong'. The institution and all the mechanisms that underpin that bullshit ridden and sedentary industry are rotten to the core.

Fortunately I have no medical or clinical qualifications, I'm just a regular guy trained in engineering and engineering sciences and like most engineers I have an engaging and problem solving mind. As a regular guy, albeit with a little bit of professional training, I would respectfully suggest that having an enquiring, capable and problem solving mind is probably the most rudimentary of all mandatory requirements for all those engaged in a key service delivery profession such as the medical industry. Now clearly the back room girls and boys of that industry appear to have that predisposition because we have all witnessed the tremendous advances that have been achieved over the past fifty years or so. I'm talking here however about medical scientists and scientific medical engineers, the people we should regard as the true heroes of medicine, the men and woman who steadfastly develop new tools, new tests, new treatments, new techniques and new machines etc, for the betterment of man. However, the heroes of medicine are a stark contrast

I now know; who I am, what I am and what I can do, for I am now pain free

to the front end 'luddites' i.e. *Any Opponent of Industrial Change or Innovation* of the medical world that we the general public are unfortunately exposed to. The people that we're exposed to are only interested in one thing and one thing only: self gratification at the expense of their fellow man. I refer of course to the medical receptionist, the nurse, the general practitioner, the registrar, the specialist and the consultant. They may or may not start off life as self protectionist 'luddites' but at the point they're allowed to administer their own unique brand of divisive, destructive and judgmental clinical administration and medical butchery up the innocent public, they move into that 'luddite' mindset wholesale.

These people are guilty of crimes against humanity that simply eclipse the acts and transgressions of the worst of all ruthless dictators. They are institutionally lazy, self obsessed, greedy, serial abusers with only one thing on their agenda, self preservation of their highly inflated status within what is the devil's own institutions. Forget any waffle about the Hippocratic oath than anyone from this industry chooses to offload onto you, the bottom line for these people is themselves first, themselves second and whatever is left over; is all for themselves. These people don't solve problems, they don't hear suffering, they're not prepared to think outside of the box and why? Well because they're the wrong people for the job, the wrong people who are gaining great rewards from an industry that is rotten to the core. For anyone misfortunate enough to develop a chronic illness I've mapped the actual clinical abuse process that most people are forced to endure during the course of their chronic illness at the end of this chapter. What the process loop cannot do is qualify the simply appalling nature, neglect and abandonment anyone experiences during that process. Where the cause of desperate conditions are often written off as psychological issues and placed directly back on the shoulders of the patients, identifying them as

My body is the greatest healer of them all and my mind is its engine

the originator and hence owner of the condition in totality. That being said; it's eminently justifiable to suggest that the selection criteria for individuals entering the medical industry and the training they undergo are now by modern day standards both outdated and fundamentally flawed. Because if the selection criteria for those entering the medical industry and their subsequent training were right; then we wouldn't have such a fundamentally flawed service and individuals who go onto develop chronic illness wouldn't simply be written off. You only need to be misfortunate enough to become ill to discover just how diabolically poor, unresponsive and uncooperative this industry really is. No matter which sector you seek help from, be it either the public or the private sectors, the service is abominable. No matter whom you consult or what level that representative may be, it doesn't matter what tests you participate in or what sort of investigation you undergo. These people know very little about very little and what they do know or articulate freely to you is generally outdated, self protectionist and complete and utter rubbish with no humanistic element to it. You see:

- How can it be that we still have a sociologically biased industry that is controlled from within?

- How can it be that we still have a sociologically biased industry that protects and rewards underperformance from those who support it or are employed by it?

- How can it be that we still have a sociologically biased industry that is afraid to acknowledge advancement in thinking until that change in approach is decades old?

I now know; who I am, what I am and what I can do, for I am now pain free

- How can it be that we still have a sociologically biased industry where those who are employed in it have no idea about the majority of diseases and conditions they encounter?

- How can it be that every unexplainable condition can be written off by those within this industry as simply being of a psychological origin?

- How can it be that they're programmed as a service provider within this industry not to hear, help or support suffering and pain?

- How can it be that no matter what your own personal or professional credentials are, as soon as you engage with this industry you're immediately considered an intellectual cretin by those providing basic services within?

- How can it be that if you dare to challenge this industry from within you're immediately risking your career?

- How can it be that fighting for resolution from chronic illness can expose you to the pressure of clinical services being withdrawn from you?

My body is the greatest healer of them all and my mind is its engine

And yet they all assume the same grotesque air of arrogance about who they are and what they are and how complicated your particular situation may or may not be. This bullshit they offload is by default, simply an outdated facade designed for a bygone age when we the general public were considered as intellectually inferior to representation from this industry. But this misguided assumption still exists today to mask clear inadequacies, ignorance and fragile egos yet the reality is that it's probably more disrespectful to us now than it ever was because we're all much smarter than this industry gives us credit for. This crux of my irritation is that this industry and those who support it are an affront to everything that is both decent and good in our modern world. We don't expect or accept bullshit and ridicule from any other private sector or public service industry. So why do we accept this institutional misconduct from the clinical world?

Well, the truth is that we really don't think that we have any power to change our situation and at the point we commence any social intercourse with this industry we're already in a state of vulnerability and low vitality. Therein resides the reason why so many people with undiagnosed disease states go onto to develop chronic illness before ultimately being written off as a neurotic or a depressive with no possible chance of making an effective recovery. You see the medical/clinical industry is very adept at falsely blaming the symptoms of chronic disease states and ultimately chronic illness upon the fragile psychology of any mortal who presents with such appalling and life debilitating conditions. But what is the truth behind this predisposition of our psychology being the root cause of all our chronic illness and chronic illness expression? Well I'm going to look at that very point in the next chapter so please fasten your seat belt, but first check out the clinical abuse loop.

I now know; who I am, what I am and what I can do, for I am now pain free

Raphael's Treatment Protocol

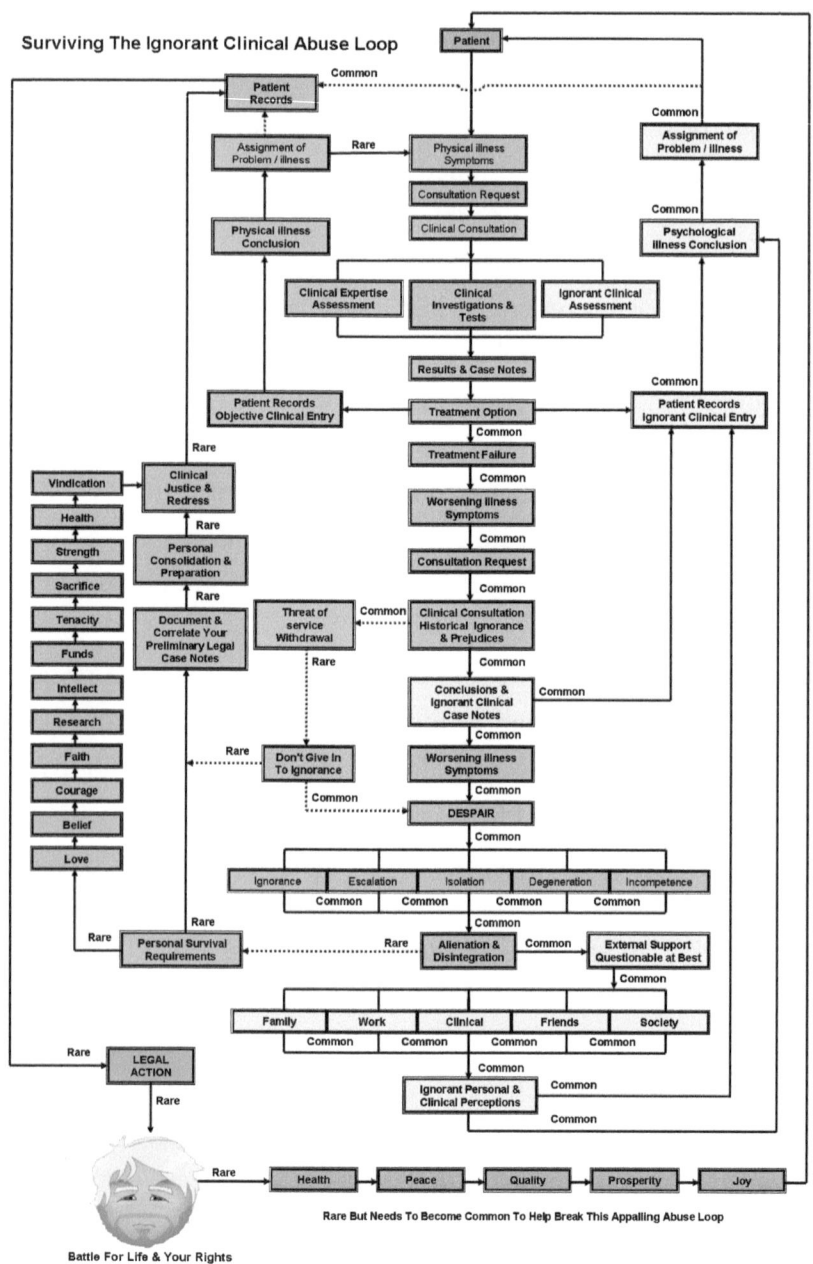

My body is the greatest healer of them all and my mind is its engine

Personal Notes

I now know; who I am, what I am and what I can do, for I am now pain free

Personal Notes

My body is the greatest healer of them all and my mind is its engine

EXPLORING PSYCHOLOGICAL ILLNESS PRAGMATICALLY

Exploration Three

I now know; who I am, what I am and what I can do, for I am now pain free

My body is the greatest healer of them all and my mind is its engine

How frequent is it for patients' problems to be simply written off as nothing more than a deluded psychology? Well far more frequently than you may expect. You see, there is a prescriptive culture within the medical world which has a predisposition for looking to offload all the patients' problems back onto them. It's basically part of the overall clinical abuse model and its guiding principles are no more than:

- When in doubt just call your patients illness a psychological problem.

- When tests don't indicate a deviation from normal values, just call your patients' illnesses a psychological problem.

- When imaging doesn't show up any abnormalities just call your patients' illnesses a psychological problem.

- When you simply can't be bothered with your patients' perceived or preposterous symptoms just call their illness a psychological problem.

I now know; who I am, what I am and what I can do, for I am now pain free

But what is the truth and just what part does our psychology play in the bigger scheme of things when it comes to our health? Well first we need to understand that whilst we may be familiar with the term 'psychological illness' few of us know that the modern day originator of this scientific field was 'Wilhelm Wundt' who established the first psychology lab in Leipzig, Germany. Believing at the time that *properly* trained individuals should be able to *accurately* identify the mental processes that accompanied an individual's feelings, sensations, and thoughts. The emphasis here is upon *properly trained* individuals accurately identifying the processes that underpin the emotional predisposition of individuals in any given psychological state.

Now the development of this science didn't happen by chance, mankind in all its societies has battled throughout its entire documented history with the thorny issue of mental illness and insanity. That's why we in the United Kingdom still have such draconian measures as the 'Mental Health Act' where citizens can be sectioned and detained under said act for extended periods if they pose either a danger to others or more often than not simply a danger to themselves. Now there is absolutely no doubt that some individuals are insane, we see that in the likes of Shipman, Stalin, Hitler and Saddam Hussein.

The problem is there have been no major advances since time began to delineate between organic insanity and biologically insults that have the propensity to inflict insanity upon mankind. So we still have no way of knowing who's insane and who's simply biologically ill. I'm advocating therefore that the golden psychological card which is so readily used to explain the unexplainable illness i.e. there is a significant psychological component to your illness, is simply a complete red herring in the majority of chronic illnesses.

My body is the greatest healer of them all and my mind is its engine

Those inaccurate value judgments simply have no clinical grounding upon which to base the assumptions of a psychological condition upon save for some cursory presenting symptoms.

Now it's that point of clinical evidence that I wish firstly to focus upon. You see; if you present yourself to a medic suspecting that you have let's say; possibly hypothyroidism. The first thing they will do is:

(a) Poo poo and ridicule you.

And then

(b) Perhaps agree reluctantly to give you a thyroid test.

They will then rattle on about how they couldn't possibly give you a trial of low dose thyroid medication until your tests results come back and prove that you do indeed have an issue with your thyroid. Yet the same medical practitioner within 5 minutes of another consultation will conclude with NO clinical data that you are indeed suffering from a psychological condition and therein he or she will feel eminently comfortable to prescribe anyone of a line of toxic psychiatric substances. It seems to me incredulous in the 21st century, that some unqualified cretin can make such sweeping statements about the condition of someone's psychology. More so when we realise that we pay these rogues insane salaries for the little that they do. Affording them great status to comply with the values and defining principles of the Hippocratic Oath. But my question is; do they deliver greatness for the greatness we bestow upon them? Well they're certainly paid insane salaries and afforded great status but very few of them have ever actually signed up to any form of; Hippocratic Oath. Furthermore it's fair to suggest that many of them don't actually know what the original Oath actually says despite the fact that they frequently hide behind it.

I now know; who I am, what I am and what I can do, for I am now pain free

I actually look at that point further in the chapter Hippocratic Oath Or Merely Hypocritical Froth focusing upon specifically all the medical illusions that we as a society are sold.

Nevertheless I'm going to labour my point here of psychological postulation over scientific rationale, by asking this:

- If I have an abscess inside my mouth accompanied by intolerable pain do I have an abscess and intolerable pain?

Or

- Do I have a psychological problem which is manifesting the symptoms of pain?

Well clearly it's the first bullet point not the latter unless that is you're employed in the medical world. You see, in the medical world seeing is not always believing whereas in the presence of no rationale, believing is always right. It is that preoccupation with self importance and unqualified value judgments that continues to blight our medical records and destroy our lives.

But what if I substitute abscess for undetectable anomaly generating misery and great pain that flawed tests and investigations are unable to detect. What do I have then?

- Do I have an undetectable anomaly which is causing misery and pain?

Or

- Do I have a deep seated psychological problem that is manifesting symptoms of misery and pain?

Well of course it's the latter in terms of medical rationale because; the very fact that my problem cannot be found means that it simply doesn't exist. It must therefore be a manifestation of my fragile psychology which requires no further input from them. Is it any wonder that I regard these rogues as the lowest form of life?

It's clearly apparent to me now that in bog standard, tricky or complex medical investigation situations we the patients are always to a greater extent perceived to be the responsible party for the clinical problem we're experiencing because as mere mortals we have such fragile psychologies. Surely though this situation is truly insane, how can this industry say on one hand that, unless their outdated investigation techniques are able to detect a problem then it simply doesn't exist whilst in the same breath assign clinical labels to patients with the shallowest to zero investigations of their case?

I do not argue or disagree with the fact that our psychology plays a very big part in the way we cope with, or handle our difficulties. But it is not the root cause of all mans hidden or seemingly translucent diseases and I therefore repudiate the waving of the psychological cause golden card by cretins within the medical industry.

If our psychology was the root cause of the majority of illnesses then we would be able to see for ourselves the advances in the treatment of psychological conditions over the past hundred years. Because the money we spend on this aspect of medical care via so called research and residential care etc, is simply insane. The reality to my primary postulation is quite stark and I say that because the medical industry is having a laugh. Nothing much has changed in the diagnosis and treatment of these conditions despite the oceans of scientific papers that have been written.

I now know; who I am, what I am and what I can do, for I am now pain free

There have been no major breakthroughs in clinical analysis, qualification or treatments of psychological conditions save for commercially sponsored indoctrination and use of debatably successful drugs. Now if anyone who has been put on those drugs has improved, all I can say is good for you, but for the majority of us who didn't need them in our body to solve our health condition, then I would respectfully suggest that they are:

- Dangerous

Or

- Complete waste of bloody time.

Yet the medical world's view remains without any validity that all illness derives from an emotional or mental state and that physical illness if it cannot be pinpointed simply doesn't exist. But surely these are the views of yesterday's men, the sorts who questioned the validity of;

- The shape of the earth.

- The purpose of the sun.

- The make-up of the moon.

- The relevance of the stars

They are the views of men who dared not seek to discover if the world was flat or round and who shouted heresy if a man sort to postulated different thoughts or articulated and challenged perceived truths.

My body is the greatest healer of them all and my mind is its engine

The very fact that this approach happens almost by default in clinical surgeries throughout the UK, simply validates my position that the medical world is seemingly still stuck in the dark ages, ignorant and despite its protestations, doesn't really care. Were they motor mechanics with the same approach to problems these people would be simply unemployable or even in jail e.g.

- 'I'm sorry Mr. Hardy but I couldn't find anything wrong with your car, but incidentally have you ever tried counselling, sometimes it really does help?'

Or what about this favourite one;

- 'Yes I hear what you say Mr. Hardy but that is just a sensation of knocking at the front of your car, I'm the expert here I can't find any signs of knocking so perhaps its more of a psychological issue than you think, how's your sex life by the way?'

Two months later the engine in my car implodes;

- 'Oh well these things just happen sometimes Mr. Hardy, I've checked your notes and it would appear that your tyres and exhaust were fine when you were last in here, now you're clearly agitated so I'm going to suggest that there seems more to this than just an engine in your car, do you think you need to see a psychiatrist?'

- 'Answer, no I don't think I should see a psychiatrist you bull shitting waste of space, I was in here not so long ago and I told you that there was something seriously wrong with my engine and all you did was check my bloody tyre pressure and exhaust mounting. Now I'm back here today with a damaged engine and I'm asking you this, are you a bloody mechanic mate or simply a mechanic on your great grandmothers side of your family because your technical and professional capabilities are shoddy to say the least?'

The thing is if this happened in real life we would be straight to trading standards but when it comes to the medical industry we're all very guilty of not being prepared to take those bastards on. The public at large would be shocked if they knew just how little psychological or psychiatric training non specialists in that field actually undergo before they're let loose on us.

I liken their understanding of psychological or psychiatry to that of the fat clever bastard who we've perhaps sat next to as lovers of football in the football stands all around our country. You know the one I mean. From beginning to end he hurls his abuse and yet he's probably never played the beautiful game. Yet he's somehow deluded himself into thinking that he's some kind of football guru.

Well, the truth is that the average medic you will ever encounter has little to no training in either psychological or matters of psychiatry and as such are the least qualified of clinicians to prescribe conditions of that nature to you or about you. Yet they have bought into ignorant schools of thought which date way back to the 1920's.

My body is the greatest healer of them all and my mind is its engine

Outdated schools of thought that postulated that we, as individuals, are responsible for all our own thoughts and our perceptions on life and that we all have demons and un-reconciled issues deep within us that frequently manifest themselves as illness. Today that belief is still perpetuated by our ignorant medics as a way of offloading the cause of a tricky problem back onto the shoulders of its originator simply because they know that they can do that.

So much so that you can bet your last £10 that if you encounter any extended or unexplainable medical issue at any point in your life, that the psychological postulations or dogma that will be rolled out or recorded on your medical records will be a derivative of some unqualified cretins understanding of:

- Personality Psychology – This specialist area looks at the various elements that make up individual personalities and includes Freud's structural model of personality as an example of a protagonist of this field.

However at the point a qualified psychologist is brought onto your case I can guarantee you that Personality Psychology which has already been used by medical ignoramuses as ammunition against you will be almost entirely dropped in favour of:

- Clinical Psychology Investigations – This specialty area is focused on the assessment, diagnosis, and treatment of mental disorders.

I now know; who I am, what I am and what I can do, for I am now pain free

However the study of psychology has moved on tremendously since its conception and there are now many widely differing schools of thought and differing approaches to this challenging subject including:

- Cognitive Psychology - This specialist area is the study of human thought processes and cognitions, including topics such as attention, memory, perception, decision-making, problem solving, and language acquisition.

- Abnormal Psychology - This specialty area is focused on research and treatment of a variety of mental disorders and is linked to psychotherapy and clinical psychology.

- Social Psychology - This specialist area is a discipline that uses scientific methods to study social influence, social perception, and social interaction. Social psychology studies diverse subjects including group behaviour, social perception, leadership, nonverbal behaviour, conformity, aggression, and prejudice.

- Comparative Psychology - This specialist area is the branch of psychology concerned with the study of animal behaviour, believing that the study of animal behaviour can lead to a deeper and broader understanding of human psychology.

- Forensic Psychology - This specialist area is an applied field focused on using psychological research and principles in the legal and criminal justice system.

- Industrial-Organizational Psychology - This specialist area uses psychological research to enhance work performance, select employee, improve product design, and enhance usability.

- Developmental Psychology - This specialist area is the branch of psychology that looks at human growth and development over the lifespan. Theories often focus on the development of cognitive abilities, morality, social functioning, identity, and other life areas.

- School Psychology - This specialist area is the branch of psychology that works within the educational system to help children with emotional, social, and academic issues.

- Biological Psychology - This approach is the only area of accessible psychology that studies how biological processes influence the mind and behaviour.

Ironically though; Biological Psychology will never be rolled out unless you've been through surgery, a crash or a smash. Yet this approach is the only area of accessible psychology that studies how biological processes influence the mind and behaviour. Now there's no getting away from it *Biological Psychology* is still light years away from where it should be by now but at least it's sort of heading in the right direction. The only problem is as ever when undergoing medical interventions, your future will depend entirely upon the training of the psychologist responsible for driving any biological investigations. You may well find that in most instances he or she just simply reverts back to or refers you to another Clinical Psychologist on the grounds of costs or insufficient evidence to warrant extensive testing.

I now know; who I am, what I am and what I can do, for I am now pain free

Throughout my darkest days I battled like a Spartan albeit a very ill Spartan to find the root cause of my illness and I was frequently told by medical representatives, 'no we're not testing you for this or for that'. Or 'we can't keep on testing for different things indefinitely Mr. Hardy you're simply going to have to understand that you have a psychiatric problem'.

Now there is absolutely no doubt that if we feel low it's difficult for us to feel happy until we shift our mind set. We see that day after day in the emotions and moods of ourselves and our kith and kin. It's simply preposterous to suggest to someone who is ill that if they change their mindset things somehow will resolve and they will feel better.

You see; life as we know is not like that, we are not like that, there are always impositions placed upon our bodies which make it impossible for us to feel happy simply as and when we choose to feel happy. The best we can ever hope to do is to recognise and accept that we have a part to play in that process yet understand that we do not always hold all the keys. So the question remains, is 'psychological illness real or simply a medical form of illness fiction?'

Well there's no doubt in my mind that there are many forms of psychological illness, but in the absence of firm biological data I cannot accept or agree that psychological illness is an illness in its own right. If the root course of a problem cannot be qualified then it MUST fall into the category of symptoms from an unknown disease. Therein there must be a concerted effort made to search out the origin of that disease and not simply to attempt to treat the symptoms with dangerous views, perceptions or drugs. Under no circumstance can an unknown disease be morally written off as an emotional or psychological illness because I would respectfully suggest that act in itself constitutes gross clinical malpractice.

My body is the greatest healer of them all and my mind is its engine

I therefore advocate that anyone being written off by a medical representative, must document that incident via a formal communiqué to their practice in readiness for future legal action. It is only at the point we start bringing the medical industry to account, day after day that we will:

- Get the services we so desperately need.

And

- Weed out the 'luddites, rogues and charlatans' who shouldn't be in the industry in the first place.

The global market place we live and work in is full of medics desperately looking to explore new boundaries. So if we don't have the quality home grown medics that we need who are prepared to accept that we're all part of the 21st century. Then I say, lets simply offload the; 'luddites, rogues and charlatans' to the unemployed wastelands where they belong and lets import brighter, fresher service support professionals as we would do with plumbers, builders, electricians and engineers.

You see; as a former sufferer of all that's wrong with our insidiously flawed medical model we simply don't have the time, money or resolve to bring the luddite bastions of our medical industry kicking and screaming into line with our modern needs, standards and expectations.

We need effective medical services now, not light years from now, but tomorrow, or at the very latest the early part of next week. What's more we can all play our part in bringing about change; help create a medical model that is technically competent, robust and able to meet ALL our needs. Start today, and let's hope that no one ever has to document the level of personal suffering that I've been forced to document and voice via *Raphael's Legacy* etc.

My body is the greatest healer of them all and my mind is its engine

EXPLORING PERSONAL MIND ANGER PRAGMATICALLY

Exploration Four

I now know; who I am, what I am and what I can do, for I am now pain free

My body is the greatest healer of them all and my mind is its engine

You know I've encountered many many very special people in my life and I'm incredibly grateful for the interactions that I've had with them all. I've been blessed to meet fine tradesmen, carers, beggars, artists, clergymen, engineers, bus drivers, road sweepers, teachers, librarians, sportsmen etc., to name just a few. Each one special and unique in their own right, each one bringing something special to my life and yet I can count on one hand the medics I've met whom I would bestow the accolade of special upon.

Yet I make no secret of the fact that whilst I will be as gracious as circumstances dictate when interacting with members of the medical industry. I nevertheless have absolutely no respect for that industry or the views of those employed within it for unless I meet a medic who is able to speak or offer a service from a point of true expertise and I don't mean legitimized bullshit. Then I'm simply not interested in what any medic has to say, and I mean, I'm not interested in anything they have to say on health, politics or any major imposition on life.

I now know; who I am, what I am and what I can do, for I am now pain free

You see, as far as I'm concerned they are the lowest of all mortal forms of life. The way these people conduct themselves, fail and abuse people in their care is a scandal and disgrace and for that I'm adamant that for their crimes against humanity they must pay a very heavy price, be that in this life or the next I really don't care. Until that happens I think its fine to explore in your head exactly what you would do to the rogues who've abused and failed you if you ever got the chance to deliver your own unique and personal retributions.

Now whilst some may say: *'Oh dear it's important for our souls and our recovery that we must let go of hatred and anger towards others'*. My answer is simply this, *'Explore that position again when you're tormented by a toxic liver, a toxic body and when every system and organ in your body has been damaged by an insidious bacteria, when it all could have been so easily prevented'* and then I would urge you to simply think your belief structures over again.

You see I personally believe that it's actually extremely healthy and positive to exercise your liver and brain anger. To explore just how far your emotions take you and what you think is suitable, punishment or not, for the suffering you've endured. Who knows, the very fact that you're prepared to explore those thoughts whilst accepting them for what they are, may just be an essential component of your recovery and a vital process that must not be ignored.

With that point of view in focus, I've had some lovely despicable thoughts about what I would like to do to the rogues who failed me. I so desperately want them to feel the level of pain that they create and perpetuate for people like me every minute of every day of their career. I've had thoughts of rounding all medics and their families up and transferring them to great football stadiums around the country.

My body is the greatest healer of them all and my mind is its engine

Where I would strap the medics into chairs and make them watch their loved ones being torn apart without mercy by Hyenas. Now obviously that would take some time because there's only so much a Hyena can eat at any given time but that's okay, the longer the suffering for all concerned the better as far as I'm now concerned. You may ask why I chose Hyenas not lions, tigers, wolfs or bears, well it's because of all the big carnivores the Hyena is in my opinion the cruelest of them all. They don't waste energy killing their victims they simply rip them apart limb from limb. I think being eaten alive and enduring unbelievable suffering before death is fine for the sort of people that I have in mind.

Now of course and after a few years naturally there wouldn't be any family or loved ones left to brutalize, so I would turn my attention directly to the medics. At which point I really would enjoy playing mind games with them torturing them day after day for years. I would inject them with all sorts of substances and break the odd one or two limbs. There would be no quarter given, no repose on grounds of mercy.

But I might allow the odd one of two to read a few books on psychology if they felt it would help them deal or cope with their physical and emotional pain. I would inject some with Lymes Disease, some with HIV, some with syphilis and some with a blend of all three. But before all of that I would revel in playing games with their head and simply talk infinitum about a whole host of things I was planning to do.

I now know; who I am, what I am and what I can do, for I am now pain free

The key in all my punishment regimes would be the generation of intolerable isolation, desolation and despair, creating a situation devoid of any humanistic sympathy or due diligence and care. In fact to replicate the culture that these rogues have rolled out on us for years, only in my regime there would be no 'DSBL's' written, no bullshit spoken and no postulation of care, my open and honest policy would be one of simple retribution and payback for the insidious lives that they'd lived.

Now I'm not sure if my anger towards the medical industry will ever subside but what matter that, all that I know is that I can't possibly allow my hatred of them to hold me back. I'm no longer their victim or some innocent that they can indiscriminately abuse, for I'm now 'Barry Hardy' the battle hardened medic hater who will delight in pursuing legal retribution and in due course regardless of whatever form or format that takes.

You see; I want everyone who's ever been chronically ill yet failed by the medical industry to realise and accept fully that they themselves were never to blame. In accepting that they, like me can exercise the demons that reside deep within us all after years of suffering. Because in accepting and not fighting our mind anger, I firmly believe that we're actually setting ourselves free. Simply because personal exploration as far as I'm concerned is nothing more than an intuitive expansive trait and if we choose to live in expansive state we very often leave our pain and suffering behind.

My body is the greatest healer of them all and my mind is its engine

Now, let me make myself clear, I would never advocate actual violence against any medical service sector worker, rogues though they are by default. Nevertheless I certainly believe and therefore think that it's healthy and positive to accept and explore our brain and liver anger because it has a vital part to play in anyone's recovery.

My only footnote would be in closing this chapter is; go gentle into that vile place and never allow yourself to be completely consumed by your cruel thoughts, just accept them for what they are.

It really is okay to hate your medical abusers and accept that they are complete 'shits, cretins and clowns'. It's okay to hate their husbands, wives and kids for reaping great rewards from being associated with and/or to those rogues.

The only point I would make is turn that hatred into positive redress and legal action and don't let it just fester or simply evaporate away. Make your formal complaints if that's what you need to do for in doing so you will kick start a myriad of much needed karmic events.

Network with fellow mindsets and empower yourself in firm assurance that you're no longer that lone foot soldier that you'd lead yourself to believe you are, because at the point you empower your psyche to engage in seeking redress, you've morphed into a dynamic and cataclysmic particle of change.

That will prove to you once and for all, that you're a very real, dramatic, even majestic vanquisher of what is an insidious blight upon society i.e. our shockingly poor and unresponsive medical model, industry and the shits who work within it who are happy to destroy far too many peoples' lives.

I now know; who I am, what I am and what I can do, for I am now pain free

My body is the greatest healer of them all and my mind is its engine

EXPLORING TREATMENT OPTIONS PRAGMATICALLY

Exploration Five

I now know; who I am, what I am and what I can do, for I am now pain free

My body is the greatest healer of them all and my mind is its engine

It was during the worst points in my illness when I discovered that orthodox medical clinicians seemed to be amongst the most technically ignorant so called professionals I'd ever encountered in my life. Nevertheless, there are some men and women of science on the fringe of that industry trying their level best to help people and to move the science of medicine along from the middle age culture that it remains to this day stuck in. The problem those guys face is that they are trying to change a culture that simply doesn't want to change. A position which invariably means that they are immediately referred to as quacks by their luddite medical peers, which means that being treated by them can become so much more difficult that it needs to be or should be.

Now hey I'm not saying that all pioneering clinicians are good guys because some are clearly not. I do however find it incredibly annoying to listen to incompetent orthodox clinicians rubbishing and or trying to dig dirt on people who are clinically committed to moving things forward. Whilst they themselves are responsible on a grandiose scale for legitimised medical genocide of the majority of people entrusted into their care. It is this macrobiotic and immutability of the medical industry that is really holding clinical treatment progress back. You see; here is an endemic culture of assumption within the medical industry which on the one hand prescribes as it sees fit, whilst on the other simply attacks and criticizes alternative approaches, based upon nothing than prejudices or personal understandings or assumptions. In the absence of clinical data they will cry foul, yet in the presence of flawed historical orthodox clinical data they will defend it to the hilt.

You only have to listen to, speak to, or be spoken to by an individual from the medical industry to appreciate just how technically incompetent they can be. How full of their own self importance they are and how intransigent they are to change and new ideas. Therefore is it any wonder then that the average clinician is reluctant to engage with new ideas, for to do so would immediately subject them to a level of scrutiny from their peers that they're simply not moralistically or intellectually able to defend?

It's for that reason and that reason only that we, as chronically ill people, must accept that when we engage in clinical dialogue with pioneers in the old fields of medical science, that both we and they are going to be ridiculed by any luddite we encounter along the way.

My body is the greatest healer of them all and my mind is its engine

You see, medical pioneering history is littered with victims of the systemically hypocritical and undoubtedly fear based corrupt judicial medical culture that appears to be hell bent upon stifling innovation. Where a preoccupation with the intentions, integrities and intellects of pioneering individuals have been brought into question and careers have been wrecked simply because some deviants are hell-bent on preventing clinical progression. Yet in far too many instances perhaps even after the pioneers' death the validity of what they were saying is later and often proven to be true.

I would therefore suggest that there has to be something fundamentally wrong with this industry and our society when:

- A clinician trying to move the envelope of medical science and clinical care forward has a proportionally greater chance of being medically disciplined or struck off, than some incompetent practitioner who's well known by his peers as being negligent in all that he or she does.

You see, I have nothing but praise for the clinical practitioners that I've met who:

- Listen.

- Treat holistically.

- Are prepared to explore new ways of being.

I now know; who I am, what I am and what I can do, for I am now pain free

You see; it's that approach and those sorts of people who will eventually change the lot of mankind for the better. Not the bullshitting cretins we encounter through our TV's or the pompous, arrogant, nasty, vindictive and incompetent rogues that we visit when we're in a state of disease. My chronic illness and the complete lack of clinical support at my disposal meant that I was forced to explore and self-fund many treatment protocols. That's why I feel it's only right that I document one or two of the treatments I explored if only to stimulate thought.

My body is the greatest healer of them all and my mind is its engine

Pyrrole Disorder

Prior to my Lymes Disease diagnosis, I make no secret of the fact that I've suffered from chronic suicidal depression and suggest that there can't possibly be anything worse than depression when absolutely nothing helps to remove or suppress its symptoms. Such was my physiological and emotional despair that I felt I needed to explore Pyroluria, a genetic condition that exhibits a wide range of symptoms most of which I'd had in the past or was suffering from at the time I explored this condition including:

- Episode of psychosis and suicidal depression.

- Little or no dream recall.

- White spots on finger nails.

- Poor morning appetite +/- tendency to skip breakfast.

- Morning nausea.

- Pale skin +/- poor tanning +/- burn easy in sun.

- Sensitivity to bright light.

- Hypersensitive to loud noises.

- Reading difficulties (e.g. dyslexia).

- Poor ability to cope with stress.

- Mood swings or temper outbursts.

I now know; who I am, what I am and what I can do, for I am now pain free

- Histrionic (dramatic).

- Argumentative/enjoy argument.

- Higher capability & alertness in the evening.

- Poor short term memory.

- Abnormal body fat distribution.

- Dry skin.

- Anxiousness.

- Significant growth after the age of sixteen.

Originally Pyroluria was known as malvaria which is a genetic abnormality in heamoglobin synthesis resulting in a deficiency of zinc and vitamin B6. People with pyroluria produce excess amounts of a by-product from hemoglobin synthesis, called OHHPL (hydroxyhemop pyrrolin-2-one). In these people an excess amount of pyrrole is found in the urine. Associated changes in fatty acid metabolism lead to low levels of arachidonicacid *an omega-6 fatty acid.* The presence of pyroluria can have a profound effect on mental and physical health and was first discovered in relation to schizophrenia. Now that's the science, here's the practicalities of the condition, you will not get tested or treated for Pyroluria on the NHS. You will need to test and pay privately via either hair or urine analysis should you decided to check for this condition. My only words of caution are that this condition is real and I tested positive for it, however;

- Finding a responsive service provider is difficult; I lost my temper and composure completely with the slow turn around in my results i.e. 8 weeks which is completely unacceptable when we are in a chronic state of suicidal expression through disease.

- I've subsequently discovered issues with my body's methylation cycle which makes treating pyroluria complicated and although I didn't know it at the time it certainly explains why my treatment of pyroluria failed.

- Advocating my recovery theme that symptoms are nothing more than the presentation of disease, I think it's important to undergo more detailed investigation before attempting to treat or stabilise pyroluria symptoms.

I now know; who I am, what I am and what I can do, for I am now pain free

Personal Notes

My body is the greatest healer of them all and my mind is its engine

Exercise, yoga and meditation etc

Prior to my chronic health condition I was a highly active guy, running the high fells every weekend, whilst during the week comfortably running in excess of fifteen miles per day on the roads, cycling, weight training and all that after a hard day's work. One of the most important aspects of that regime was the mind and body work I completed after my physical exertion, because without relaxation and bodily cleansing I found my body simply didn't work or perform in a way that I expected of it and dare I say in my ignorance; demanded of it at times.

Yet some people never get this subtle recovery nuance, thinking that exercise in itself at whatever cost, is more than enough for a happy healthy life. However, if your body is in a diseased state or exhausted, then your bodily processes either slow down or give up the fight completely, at which point its easy for all of us to lose all sense of quality in life. Therefore, whilst exercise and relaxation are essential components of optimum health, I would nevertheless suggest that those suffering from chronic illness exercise with extreme caution. Because when our body is in a diseased or a fatigued state it simply:

- Stops producing the products required to assist with bodily repair or toxin detoxification.

And

- Stops producing the energies we need to support the basic demands of living a normal healthy life.

I now know; who I am, what I am and what I can do, for I am now pain free

Therefore, anything that puts either an unnecessary or greater strain on those processes is not helpful. In fact it could actually begin to compromise any effort you make to try to recover from your chronic health condition.

You see, our bodies must be able to recover from any physical load we place upon them no matter how gentle or therapeutic an activity is perceived e.g. yoga. A failure to understand this basic principle will leave you feeling constantly fatigued and ill, which is not in your long term recovery interests at all.

Therefore despite populist agendas which state that, when we're chronically ill, pursuit of activities such as yoga are actually good for us, as someone who's been chronically ill myself, I must and do fervently disagree. My personal experiences dictate that in the majority of instances exercise of any predisposition is counter-productive to healing at best and quite dangerous at worst, until our bodies have begun, through proactive intervention, the process of invigorated self-healing. I therefore would urge anyone suffering or recovering from a chronic illness NOT to explore physical exercise in any way shape or form until that is their body is well enough to deal with such demands.

My body is the greatest healer of them all and my mind is its engine

Personal Notes

I now know; who I am, what I am and what I can do, for I am now pain free

Vitamins & Amino Acids

I don't think there is a vitamin, mineral, amino acid, superfood, glandular, herb or supplement that I haven't taken in the past thirty years. Such has been my devotion to the pursuit of wellness that numerous health food shop owners have actually known me by my first name and have even asked me in many instances for feedback on the rarer products I've tried. I've shipped products to the UK from all around the world and yet I've never found one single product or associated treatment protocol that did what its hype postulated it was capable of doing.

Now there are many reasons for that, but the fact of the matter is that if we decided to take supplements, then we must be able to determine when they are working and when they are causing rebound side effects. I've had simply hundreds of harrowing experiences on my road to recovery but the one that sticks clearly in my mind is my desperate attempts to stabilise my depression by attempting to adhere to the key principles of the 'Mood Cure'.

The Mood Cure is a protocol which postulates a comprehensive natural approach to stabilising moods through the ingestion of amino acids combined with a high-protein, healthy-fat, veggie-rich diet and other nutritional strategies. The key component of this protocol being, a four-part questionnaire designed to identify your mood type, therein once qualified mapping an appropriate treatment strategy designed to raise your mood. Now there is some legitimacy with some of the issues raised with this approach, but its biggest failing is that it attempts to treat symptomology and in my opinion completely ignores the root cause determination of disease.

My body is the greatest healer of them all and my mind is its engine

It's for that reason that I advocate that approaching this protocol unsupervised is dangerous, for it's eminently possible to exacerbate your mood symptoms and find yourself in a deeper black hole. I've accelerated my thought processes beyond imagination, I've lowered my mood significantly, I've made myself hyper and I've made myself sombulant using products prescribed via the mood cure, yet I have no idea if that was because of my underlying disease state or not.

What I do know is that whilst The Mood Cure is very informing, it falls short of a holistic treatment protocol the reason being: it focuses almost entirely upon brain function with some in put about the adrenals, but ignores other possible origins of disease. That is it's failing as far as I'm concerned simply because it does not attempt to address holistically via scientific or clinical root cause analysis other disease states that can propagate shifts in our mood and/or lead to chronic depression expression at any point in our lives.

I now know; who I am, what I am and what I can do, for I am now pain free

Personal Notes

My body is the greatest healer of them all and my mind is its engine

Counselling

Having studied psychology for the best part of my adult life, there are not many counselling techniques that I've not studied, participated in or read about. The result of which is that I understand that it's very easy to either react and deny ownership of our emotions or drill down into them and analyse them to the far end of a fart. Safe to say that as a guy committed to my own development I underwent extensive personal counselling before my pre-diagnosed Lymes Disease which was driving me around the bend. Yet in all my dealings in this area I've only ever met two counsellors that I respected, because they were real people, they'd been through the mill themselves and yet they'd come through and out the other side.

The rest have been intellectual game playing cretins, complete bullshit merchants, hypocrites or charlatans of the highest order. So much so that I now advise anyone attending counselling to sit up and take note. If you're leaving a counselling session lower than you were before you went in, then the first thing you must do is cancel any further counselling session because it's not working or the counsellor hasn't got a clue. Either that or your organic diseased state is interfering with the process.

My view is as I've stated many times in this book, our thoughts are a product of our body's chemical process efficiencies. If something is affecting them, then our thoughts will not improve until we correct those processes. Anyone that's truly been through a major chronic emotional or depressive cycle will know that it's simply impossible to change your thoughts.

I now know; who I am, what I am and what I can do, for I am now pain free

That is the major stumbling block that I have with counselling. I disagree that the mind can cure or resolve a chronic diseased state, but once the chronic diseased state has been tackled, then the mind can certainly help with a holistic recovery. So if you're thinking about attending counselling as a means of trying to recover from chronic illness, I would say think again and only do so if you're 100% sure that the origin of your symptoms are emotional and not simply diseased state generated emotional symptomology. But you'll only know that for sure once you've tested and ruled out organic disease in the first place.

My view is *'Our mind is the victim of our toxic bodily load, it does not self generate toxic emotions or toxic thoughts, our mind is as happy and free as a bird at the point that we address all our body's toxic load'.*

My body is the greatest healer of them all and my mind is its engine

Personal Notes

I now know; who I am, what I am and what I can do, for I am now pain free

Hormone Replacement

When our bodies are under attack by illness or the sheer ferocity of life there is always the potential for our hormonal system to break down. When that happens we are presented with all sorts of physiological and emotional challenges which can be difficult at best and life sapping at worst. Facing that situation there is enough evidence to suggest that supplementation with small amounts of hormones and/or their precursors can be beneficial. Because of that I don't think there is a hormone or hormone precursor that I haven't taken in the past thirty years.

Now whilst I would never contest low dose supplementation of hormones and/or hormone precursors if an individual felt the need to do that, because I have received benefits from supplementing with low dose prednisolone, cortef and armour myself. I do through personal experience suggest that supplementing with pregnenolone, estrogens, (oestrogens) testosterone, DHEA and progesterone etc., should be avoided if at all possible. I say that simply because I've self supplemented with all the former hormones and to be honest it can be a very scary and unforgiving experience.

What's even more disturbing is that supplementing with low dose hormones and/or their precursors from my own personal experience actually exasperated my illness expressions. Therefore I would say to anyone interested in exploring supplementing with hormones and/or their precursors, take it very slowly, be sure of your research and above all; listen, monitor and record your physiological and emotional responses continuously. If you adhere to those simple guidelines you can ensure that at all times you're in total control.

My body is the greatest healer of them all and my mind is its engine

Personal Notes

I now know; who I am, what I am and what I can do, for I am now pain free

Thyriod / Adrenals

For me the endocrine system plays a significant part in chronic illness and I was lucky because I met some very decent private clinicians as I battled to stabilise my well being. Whilst there is absolutely no doubt that supervised support of the adrenals and thyroid can certainly help some conditions. There are significant issues globally with the treatment of endocrine issues such as hypothyroidism and hypoadrenalism and it is certainly possible to treat those conditions to good effect.

However, support of the endocrine system is not the great panacea that some people have been lured into believing. Inspirational success stories like Diane Holmes and her book *'Tears Behind Closed Doors'* have created buy in to these conditions to the detriment of conclusive clinical investigations. When I was exploring hypothyroidism it was simply desperate reading online, people trying to emulate Diane by medicating with Thyroxine or Armour yet unable to make any progress.

It was only as I began to bottom out my own illnesses that I realised why that was. You see, whilst the thyroid might be underperforming it should not be simply taken for granted that all associated symptoms are directly attributable to thyroid malfunction. The key for me is, support your thyroid and adrenals if you feel you need to, but if you're not improving then you need to test for possible originating diseases because it may well be that it's the diseases that are challenging your endocrine system and not your endocrine systems that is in a diseased state.

My body is the greatest healer of them all and my mind is its engine

Personal Notes

I now know; who I am, what I am and what I can do, for I am now pain free

Massage & Heller Work

As a committed amateur sportsman I always understood the significant part that sports and remedial massage played in my physical performance both as a footballer and runner. It has to be one of the best ways there is to help push the debris of exercise out of your tissues and into your lymphatic system. During my chronic illness however I spent thousands of pounds on remedial massage, desperately trying to get some degree of flexibility again back into my legs, arms, back, shoulders and neck. All to no avail, my muscles would begin to lock up again in most instances before I'd even left the treatment room.

It's absolutely insane the number of medical personnel who wrote me off with stress and the number of clinicians who did the exact same thing as Lymes Disease destroyed, through neurotoxicity induced inflammation, all flexibility in my body. That is the point I need to make, if massage is unable to relax your muscles, ignore any comments about your body being in a state of stress, you must test and continue to test for originators of disease e.g. Lymes Disease etc, until you find your answer.

Because there is absolutely no way that your body can fail to respond to massage if you're simply suffering from stress in the form of adrenal insufficiency.

My body is the greatest healer of them all and my mind is its engine

Personal Notes

I now know; who I am, what I am and what I can do, for I am now pain free

Samento

When I was diagnosed with Lymes Disease, samento was the first natural product that I was prescribed and it really did have a tremendous impact in terms of killing lymes. Samento's beneficial properties are mainly attributed to a group of actives called pentacyclic oxindole alkaloids (POA's) that act on the cellular immune system. In most Cat's Claw species, the presence of another group, the tetracyclic oxindole alkaloids (TOA's) greatly inhibits the action of the POA's yet Samento is certified to be 100% TOA free.

What does all that mean? Well it means that Samento is extremely potent, you only need to take small amounts of it to ensure that its antimicrobial effects kick in. Whilst that may sound great in the treatment of lymes, it is but equally its not. You see, the problem with Lymes Disease is that it disrupts lots of systems in the body ultimately disabling the bodies detoxing capabilities. This means that whilst you kill the Lymes Disease when taking samento, the probability is that your condition will not be significantly improved because the byproduct of that treatment regime is a ten fold increase in your mobile/circulating neurotoxin load.

In conclusion whilst Samento has a part to play if you choose to use it in your recovery from lymes. Simply supplementing with it will not bring about any form of recovery unless your detox capabilities are first enhanced and supported through your entire treatment protocol for life.

Personal Notes

I now know; who I am, what I am and what I can do, for I am now pain free

Antibiotics

When herbal treatments didn't bring about the sort of recovery I needed from my Lymes Disease I explored orthodox medications such as antibiotics. Despite what you may read or be told that Lymes Disease can be cured with a short course of doxycycline, amoxicillin or minocycline, I'm clinically advising you now as a chronic lymes sufferer such statements are misleading and absurdly wrong wrong wrong. What they are capable of doing within days is to create a wide range of side effects including ototoxicity of the inner ear. That may mean nothing to you, but it should because it is irreversible damage to your inner ear and could result in you having to cope with rotary vertigo for the rest of your life as well as trying to cope with lymes.

My view is for chronic conditions such as Lymes Disease, stay as far away from antibiotics as you possibly can. There may be a place for them in other situations, but for chronic situations they're a complete waste of space.

My body is the greatest healer of them all and my mind is its engine

Personal Notes

I now know; who I am, what I am and what I can do, for I am now pain free

Reiki & Spiritual Healing

Reiki is the name given to a system of natural healing which evolved in Japan from the experience and dedication of Dr Mikao Usui. He spent most of his life practicing and teaching Reiki. It is believed by many Reiki practitioners that it's possible to heal at any level of being, be that, physical, mental, emotional or spiritual.

Unfortunately, despite being a Reiki practitioner myself, it didn't help me, despite visiting more than a few practitioners in my pursuit of relief. Neither did spiritual healing; a situation which challenged me to my core since I had witnessed and believed in the spiritual dimension all my life. I was shocked that at my time of greatest need instead of the light forces coming in to help me it was only the dark forces that saw fit to attach themselves to me.

Now we can't be anything other than what we were born to be and I've been either cursed or blessed by the vast range and depths of powers and skills that I've experienced. All that I say on the matter of Reiki is stay open and if works for you then accept it, because if it works then as far as you should be concerned that's really okay in the greater scheme of things.

My body is the greatest healer of them all and my mind is its engine

Personal Notes

I now know; who I am, what I am and what I can do, for I am now pain free

Marshall Protocol

I tried this protocol when I was making no progress at all with my lymes treatment. The premise of the protocol is to block all inflammation process whilst killing all cellular microorganisms and bacteria's. The two hormones cited as drivers of the inflammatory process are Angiotensin II and the seco-steroid 1,25-dihydroxyvitamin-D. Blocking Angiotensin II apparently weakens immune evading bacteria to the point where they can be more easily killed, and reducing the 1,25-D makes it harder for the bacteria to slip in and out of the cells that they have infected. The angiotensin receptor blocker Olmesartan dosed approximately every six hours is used to block the Angiotensin II receptors in the inflamed tissue and small doses of Minocycline can then be ingested to finish the bacteria off. So does this treatment work? Well it certainly lowers inflammation but as far as improving health, well I'm not sure.

I didn't like the side effects of this protocol, I got to the point where I could hardly walk because of the lowering in blood pressure caused by the Olmesartan and I got very cheesed off with the vertigo cause by Minocycline.

Within a few weeks I didn't value the Marshall Protocol at all and I certainly didn't like the Marshall Protocol online culture. I would never recommend this treatment option to anyone but if people wish to explore it I would simply say to them; by all means go for it, but be careful whatever you do.

My body is the greatest healer of them all and my mind is its engine

Personal Notes

I now know; who I am, what I am and what I can do, for I am now pain free

Mickel Therapy

I explored this treatment because there was a lot of hype around it at the time I was looking for answers. The main premise of the Mickel Therapy is Hypothalamitis. The therapy postulates that when 'infected' the hypothalamus thinks the body is under attack, so it will tell the body to produce chemicals to prepare muscles for fight or flight. That's a very long winded way of saying that your endocrine system is on full alert. The therapy revolves around you listening to your body and then telling it to calm down and in doing so your body starts to heal.

Well sorry not for me I'm afraid; there's no way on this green planet that anyone suffering from a chronic degenerative illness is going to recover from this therapy. But that's not to say that it doesn't have some validity, because there appears to be enough evidence to suggest that the therapy does work for individuals suffering from mild neurosis.

So if it works for them than I say great, but I would never recommend the therapy despite Dr David Mickel coming across on the surface to me as a thoroughly decent guy.

My body is the greatest healer of them all and my mind is its engine

Personal Notes

I now know; who I am, what I am and what I can do, for I am now pain free

Homeopathy

With absolutely no faith in the medical industry I explored homeopathy because passed experiences had sort of indicated that it had some validity. Unfortunately I had prediagnosed Lymes Disease symptoms when I committed myself fully to this treatment approach and it simply failed my wholesale. My body was in a hypometabolic state which meant I reacted dreadfully to everything thing I ingested including all things homeopathic.

The result of which I have to say pushed me further into a diseased state as my adrenals etc., simply couldn't cope with the increased emotional load from its so called clearing fall out. I had many bad experiences with homeopaths and because of that I feel very strongly about some of their attitudes etc.

So if anyone from the homeopathic world ever says to you that the remedy is not responsible for the reaction your experiencing it's your body. Look them straight in the eye and ask them this, 'Did you or did you not give me a remedy' and they will naturally reply 'Yes' Your answer must then be, 'Well I took your remedy and that's why I feel like this, now can we please stop all the clap trap and bullshit, because I need some help'.

The reason that I've mentioned that is because there are some very talented homeopaths out there, but equally there are a lot of quacks and I even lived and allowed myself to be treated by a quack during the most dreadful period of and in my life. The quacks are both a danger to themselves and a danger to society and trust me on this I saw one or two full on quacks.

My body is the greatest healer of them all and my mind is its engine

Anyway enough of that, so where do I sit in terms of homeopathic treatment? Well, my view is it can't clear or help anyone with a chronic bacterial, viral, fungal or neurotoxin load. But as the condition becomes more under control, then that's the point homeopathy comes into its own, supporting the patient though there coming to terms and letting go process and in my opinion nothing more.

I believe in the power of homeopathy when used in the right situation and prescribed by a first class homeopath. But when used in the wrong situation or prescribed by 'homeo-quacks' it's very, very dangerous and a complete waste of money and time.

I now know; who I am, what I am and what I can do, for I am now pain free

Personal Notes

My body is the greatest healer of them all and my mind is its engine

CranioSacral

This therapy is a gentle, hands-on method of evaluating and enhancing the function of a physiological body system called the CranioSacral system. The CranioSacral system is comprised of the membranes and cerebrospinal fluid which form the fluid-filled sac around the core of the nervous system, surrounding, nourishing, and protecting the brain and spinal cord. Using a touch generally no heavier than the weight of a small coin, skilled practitioners can monitor this rhythm at key body areas to pinpoint the source of an obstruction or stress.

The problem with this treatment approach is that it's absolutely of no use when the body is in a diseased state such as with Lymes Disease. This is because the Lymes and its neurotoxin load just keep placing an exceptional amount of stress upon the body. Frequently I found that some CranioSacral practitioners were not able to accept that it was a disease and not me the patient who was preventing progress using this approach.

Moreover there's a practitioner whom I visited many times in the Lake District prior to my Lymes Disease diagnosis that I will gladly rip limb from limb if I ever meet him again for all the ignorant abuse he offloaded onto me. I can't believe that I paid some anal quack a lot of money, to weekly verbally abuse me about my personal psychology, citing that and it as the reason I was in such a desperate state.

I now know; who I am, what I am and what I can do, for I am now pain free

Personal Notes

My body is the greatest healer of them all and my mind is its engine

Rife Technology

Desperate to get ontop of my Lymes Disease I purchased a Rife Machine from South Africa at a cost of £1800 pounds plus import duty of £250 pounds or so. The Rife machine was developed by Dr. Royal R. Rife in the 1930s and used a variable frequency, pulsed radio transmitter to produce mechanical resonance within the cells of the physical body. The Rife machine was, in its time, a pioneering front-runner for what today is the basis of energetic medicine. Rife discovered he could use specific electro-magnetic frequencies to kill a bacteria or viruses without causing damage to the surrounding tissue.

The portable rife machines of today also work on the principle of sympathetic resonance, which states that if there are two similar objects and one of them is vibrating, the other will begin to vibrate as well, even if they are not touching. In the same way that a sound wave can induce resonance in a crystal glass and ultra-sound can be used to destroy gall-stones.

Rife machines use sympathetic resonance to physically vibrate the cells of the parasite resulting in possible elimination. Now the reason I went for a rife machine over a Dr. Hulda Clark Zapper was because nothing I'd read or heard convinced me that that the Zapper was able to create anywhere near the breadths and depths of frequencies that the modern rife machines could.

So did and does the Rife machine work? Oh yes without any shadow of a doubt, the only problem is that it kills so much lymes and interrelated organisms that the herx reactions are extremely intense. When I first started using my Rife machine I was a very ill guy yet the results of using my Rife machine simply knocked me on my back as my body was swamped with neuro and bio toxins.

I now know; who I am, what I am and what I can do, for I am now pain free

It wasn't until I'd re-energized my detox capabilities that I was able to use my Rife machine with any degree of comfort.

The really good thing about the Rife machine when using it to treat Lymes is that the Lymes cannot change its form when under attack like it does with herbs and other treatment. Because the Rife Machine simply vibrates it to death whatever forms the damn disease chooses to adopt.

Would I recommend use of a Rife machine? Well yes I would but I think I would suggest that people buy one between them and take turns rather than forking out over 2k. It's a lot of money and whilst you'll have it for years, it does a lot of sitting around when not in use and I don't think that makes for a good investment because of the initial financial expense.

My body is the greatest healer of them all and my mind is its engine

Personal Notes

I now know; who I am, what I am and what I can do, for I am now pain free

Detoxing & Blood Cleaning

There was a point in my health decline and numerous unsuccessful recovery treatment protocols that I tried many detox approaches and many blood cleaning approaches. So much so that when I look back now it's simply staggering because I never made any form of improvement for all the expense and suffering I endured. I now understand that attempting to detox via the various methods we read or see online, on TV or in magazines is simply not the right approach for chronically ill people.

You see, when we become infected with lymes or diseases of that nature, our livers and/or our overall detox capabilities are significantly damaged or compromised. That means that we move into a toxic body state because we're constantly being poisoned by the disease generated toxins that are constantly being circulating or laid down in the fat rich tissues of our body. Unfortunately the vast majority of so called detox experts don't fully understand how our body processes work beyond, the liver, gallbladder or pancreas if you're lucky.

They simply don't understand mitochondria blockage or the breakdown in methylation and sulfanation processes. They don't understand liver anger or herxing with any degree of acuity. All of them in general make ridiculous claims that after one week or one month detoxing on their regime you'll feel remarkably much better. When in fact you won't if you've got a chronic toxic body but there is a significant chance that you'll feel much worse.

My body is the greatest healer of them all and my mind is its engine

My view is simply this; explore anything and everything you wish to explore in terms of detoxing, but do not under any circumstance undergo any form of rigorous detox regime if your suffering from a chronic illness. Because the price you'll pay is far greater than you could ever know i.e. significantly increased symptomology, increase fat gain around the middle despite claims to the contrary, greater fatigue, anger, depression and no improvement at all.

Personal Notes

My body is the greatest healer of them all and my mind is its engine

Shoemaker Neurotoxin Cleanse

This treatment protocol developed by Dr. Richie Shoemaker is based around the real phenomenon of biotoxins causing continuation of illness in the majority of chronically illness patients. The protocol advocates taking the medication Questran (cholestyramine) which is powder that acts like a sponge binding circulating toxins within the body to it. Questran is often prescribed to pull cholesterol out of people's bodies and is easy to ingest.

Now I tried this protocol because I believe in Toxic Body Syndrome *TBS* but unfortunately for me it didn't work at the time although I was only given a very short prescription of Questran from my GP. Nevertheless if anyone felt that they were experiencing TBS, I would certainly suggest that they read up on the Shoemaker protocol because there is great validity in lowering toxin loads in the chronically ill.

I now know; who I am, what I am and what I can do, for I am now pain free

Personal Notes

My body is the greatest healer of them all and my mind is its engine

Sauna Therapy

In an aid to help with detoxing I underwent years of wet sauna therapy and to be honest it did absolutely nothing for me. When I switched to a Far Infra Red sauna however the results were far more dramatic, so much so that I bought one and use one to this day. The infra red sauna is cheap to run, requires only a standard electrical plug point, its easy to sit in, stimulates a significant increase in sweat and toxin mobilization and I cannot recommend it highly enough.

Like all other conjunctive therapies though it needs to be treated with respect. When using a FIR we need to support our bodies with colloidal minerals and vitamins etc., we need to hydrate and we need to make sure that the sauna is kept clean and that we shower immediately upon leaving the sauna to ensure that we minimize re-assimilation of toxins.

In summation the difference between wet and FIR saunas is that the wet penetrates the skins surface and offers very little detox support. Whereas the FIR penetrates deep into the body and mobilizes and pushes both fat and water soluble toxins out of your body and in essence reduces your overall toxic load.

I now know; who I am, what I am and what I can do, for I am now pain free

Personal Notes

My body is the greatest healer of them all and my mind is its engine

Methylation

One of the areas of research that really stimulated my interest as I desperately tried to get on top of my neurotoxin load was the issue of our methylation process. Our methylation process is the primary driving force behind so many processes in our body's attempt to detox harmful substances. Effective 'markers' for methylation are:

(a) Whole blood histamine ref. levels 40-70 mcg/dL.

And

(b) Absolute Basophils ref. levels 30-50.

In terms of determining how effective our methylation processes, are elevated histamine and/or elevated basophils by default indicate undermethylation and that's not really good news. Methylation is involved in DNA synthesis, masking and unmasking of DNA detoxification, heavy mental detoxification, nerve myelination, carnitine and coenzyme Q 10 synthesis. Therefore it's essential if we are to have good health that we have an effective methylation process. But what can we do if our methylation processes are not working? Well current thinking is that we can kick start our methylation processes with the supplementation of precursors of the methylation process including:

- Folic Acid and Vitamin B12.

- Trimethylglycine (natural sugar beet source).

- Vitamin B6 (combination of Pyridoxine HCL and Pyridoxal 5 phosphate).

I now know; who I am, what I am and what I can do, for I am now pain free

- Choline (combination of Choline bitartrate and phosphatidyl choline).

- Taurine.

- Magnesium (Magnesium Glycinate).

- Zinc (Zinc Monomethionate).

- Copper (Copper Glycinate).

Now it would be fair to assume that by supporting our methylation process with those supplements that everything would sort of resolve itself and our methylation would recover. Well that would be the case if it was as simple as that but its not and it's not because some of us have dysfunctional methylation processes from birth. So much so that if we start pushing the methylation process over and above our bodily needs we can easily push ourselves into a much more dangerous state. As I've discussed earlier undermethylation can result in high histamine which can present as:

- Obsessive-compulsive tendencies.

- Oppositional-defiant disorder.

- Seasonal depression.

All of which are associated with low serotonin levels. If we push our methylation process to much though in an attempt to improve our detoxing capabilities we can drastically reduce our histamine levels. So what you may ask that's surely a good result isn't it?

My body is the greatest healer of them all and my mind is its engine

Well in truth its most definitely not. You see, very quickly you could end up with suicidal depression amongst other things, because healthy levels of histamine are vital for so many functions in our bodies. That's why playing around un-supervised with our methylation process is unwise at best and extremely dangerous at worst; because with in a matter of days you may easily find that your thought processes are like those from another planet. In essence it's important to understand when pushing our methylation process the difference between histadelia and histadelics. So let me wrap up the biochemistry of high and low histamine so that you have a much clearer understanding of the point I'm trying to make, you see:

- Histadelia is a condition which is characterized by elevated serum levels of histamine and basophils processes similar symptoms to those covered early in pyroluria.

Whereas:

- Histadelics are people with low histamine and typical symptoms include under-achievement, more severe thought disorder and hallucinations, paranoid thoughts with less pronounced obsessions, suicidal depression, cyclic or suicidal depression, and anxiety.

Clearly therefore; when attempting to manipulate your methylation process, you must take that initiative onboard with great caution, because the dynamics of histamine balancing are extremely complex.

I now know; who I am, what I am and what I can do, for I am now pain free

Now look, I've briefly covered a number of treatment options in this chapter but to be honest, I would say to anyone thinking of undergoing any form of treatment option. Before you commence your treatment option or protocol you must make sure that:

- You understand the science behind what you're doing.

- You are sure that it's the right approach for you.

- You have appropriate clinical support.

- You're going to be able to make the decisions you may need to make if at any point complications set in for you.

Above all things take NO notice of anecdotal evidence or retorts, including any passions expressed in this book. Because you must personally prove, validate and ratify everything you're about to undertake in your treatment approach, because your wellbeing and even your life depends upon it.

The bottom line at the end of the day is that your wellbeing and future happiness rests solely and at all times with you. So be honest and true to yourself and make sure that whatever route or options you take you remain always focused and in control.

But more than just that, I wish for you the best of luck and hopefully the return to that level of health and wellbeing that we all so richly deserve.

My body is the greatest healer of them all and my mind is its engine

Personal Notes

I now know; who I am, what I am and what I can do, for I am now pain free

Personal Notes

My body is the greatest healer of them all and my mind is its engine

Personal Notes

I now know; who I am, what I am and what I can do, for I am now pain free

The key is to remember that the process of healing can be accelerated when we take control of effective root cause analysis etc, a dynamic clearly profiled in my pictorial healing times lines (a) and (b) and qualifying in (c) and (d) the dynamic of understanding whether you're on the correct treatment rationale for you or not.

You see; there are no great rewards for anyone in unnecessary suffering because it adds very little to our life at all. Therefore we must always listen to our body and our higher self and learn to understand the truth and/or substance of everything we hear, read, see or feel in our body as we pursue our quest of a greater and better quality of life. Without that personal commitment, there is no real potential for whole body healing, because the process of healing both begins and ends with our ability to self nurture, self solve and self support our bodies throughout our entire and overall healing process. Because in truth, we're the only ones who can give it our full and highly considered attention and that's because, invariably we're the only ones who truly care anyway.

My body is the greatest healer of them all and my mind is its engine

My Actual Healing Time Line
Time Line (a)

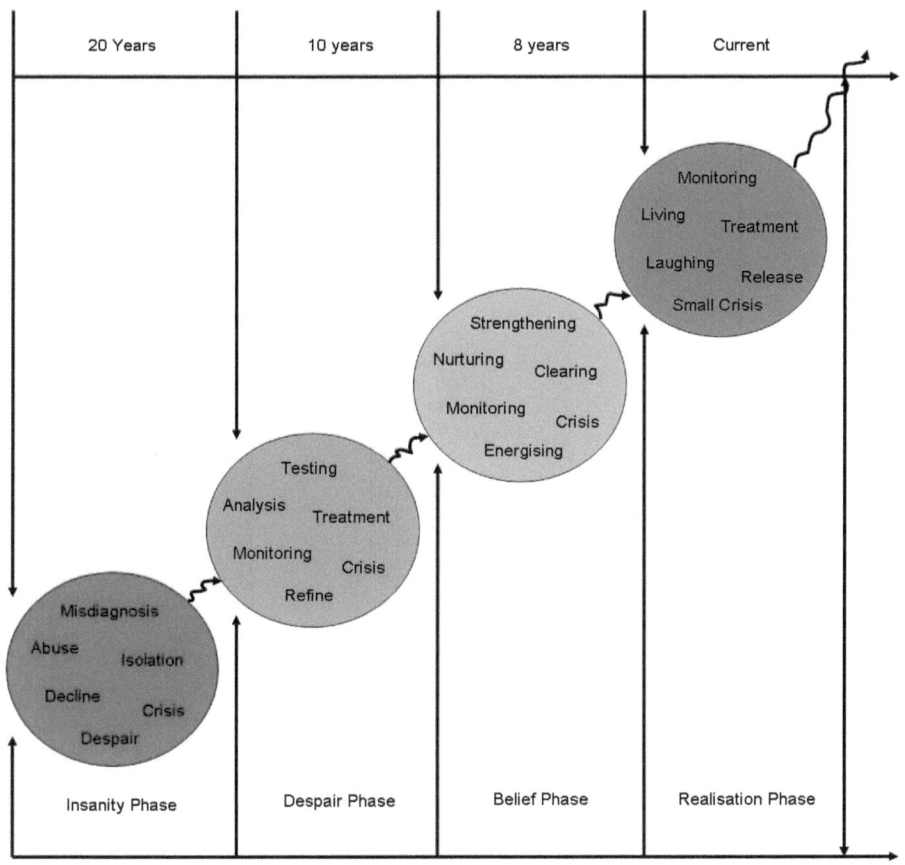

Time is only the great healer when our healing time is spent well

I now know; who I am, what I am and what I can do, for I am now pain free

Raphael's Treatment Protocol

Possible Healing Time Line
Time Line (b)

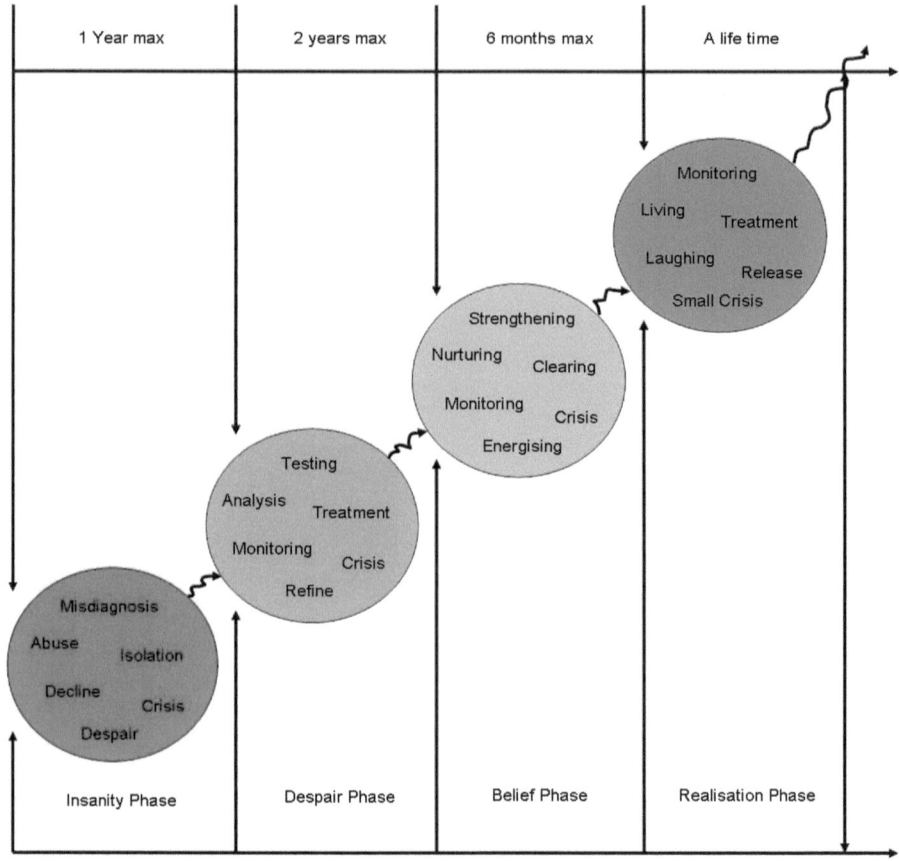

Time is only the great healer when our healing time is spent well

My body is the greatest healer of them all and my mind is its engine

Inappropriate Treatment Time Line 4U
Time Line (c)

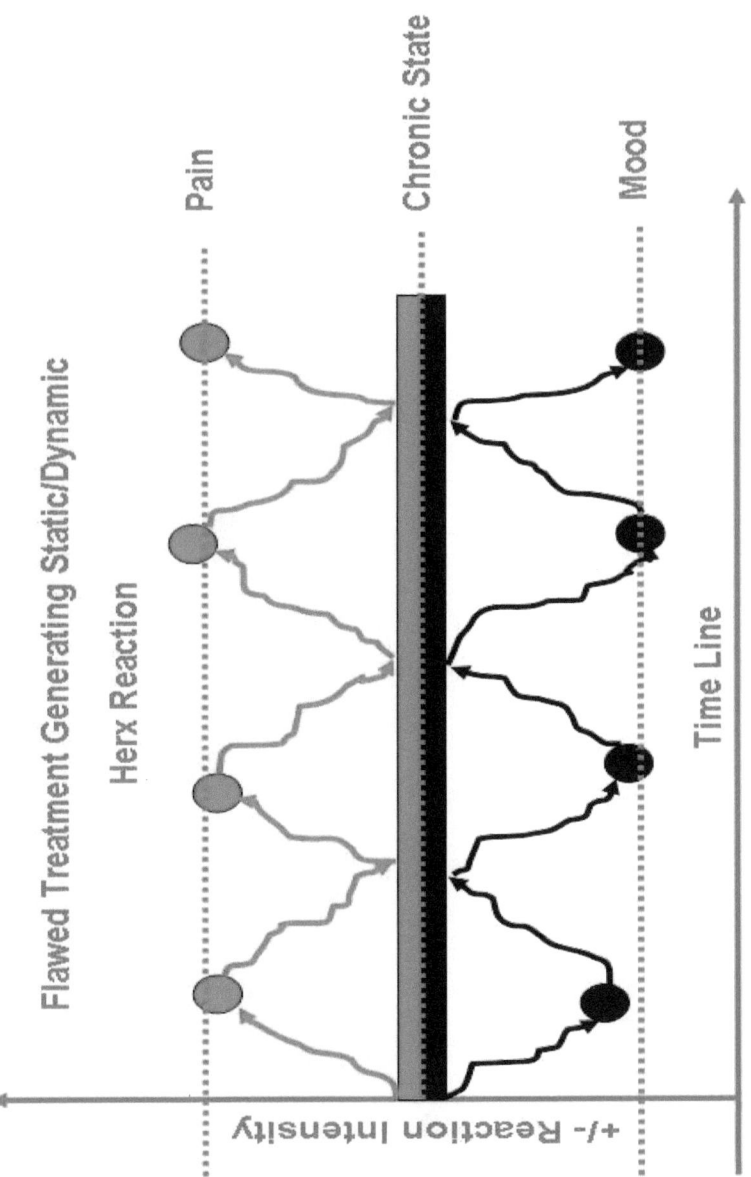

I now know; who I am, what I am and what I can do, for I am now pain free

Correct Treatment Time Line 4U
Time Line (d)

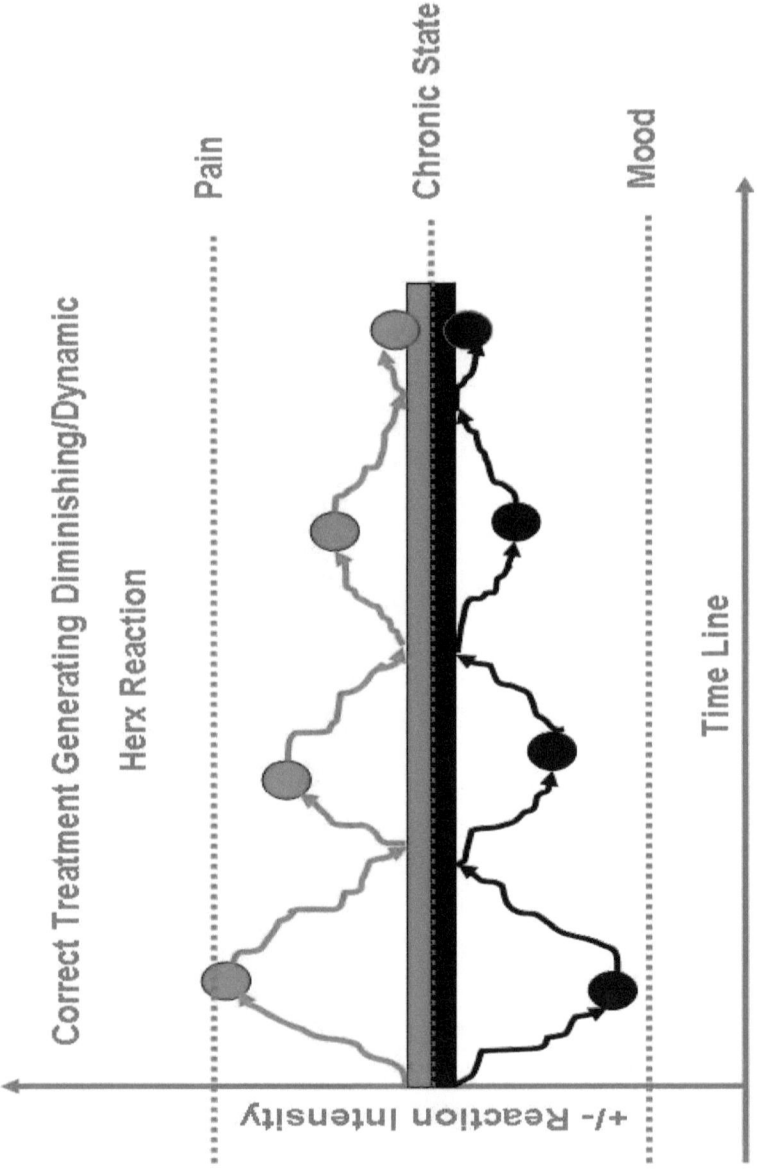

My body is the greatest healer of them all and my mind is its engine

Personal Notes

I now know; who I am, what I am and what I can do, for I am now pain free

Personal Notes

My body is the greatest healer of them all and my mind is its engine

EXPLORING THE INSANITY OF TESTING PRAGMATICALLY

Exploration Six

I now know; who I am, what I am and what I can do, for I am now pain free

My body is the greatest healer of them all and my mind is its engine

It's fair to say that some of us really go through the mill several times before our illness is finally diagnosed, yet at the point we're diagnosed we then hopefully via an effective treatment regime, can begin to make a substantive recovery from our presenting conditions. Sadly however, some of us actually never recover and that's primarily due to two reasons:

- Our condition is terminal.

- Or analytical sciences and clinical investigations are simply unable to detect a problem.

Ironically, during my baron chronic illness resolution days, whilst I was failed wholesale by UK analytical sciences and clinical investigations, I was diagnosed as terminally ill in the USA. How strange is that?

Well not that strange really when you scratch the surface of analytical sciences and clinical investigations in the UK. You see, the vast majority of tests, machines, and imaging devices that we have in the UK are not state of the art as the industry or our government would like us to believe. They're actually state of the ark. It's not until you actually analyse the state of that medical service sector that you find out just how bad things really are.

I now know; who I am, what I am and what I can do, for I am now pain free

A situation compounded further by the front end medical cretins who request investigations and then either play a part or choose to abstain from interpolating any subsequent results objectively leaving us as the sufferer bemused.

I really don't think there can be anything worse than having a major health impediment and yet because of out dated and fundamentally flawed analytical sciences and clinical investigations no one can find anything wrong with you. At that point despite your intense suffering you're simply written off as a neurotic and the most alarming thing is that there is no difference either between the NHS and the private sector.

Time after time I've paid for very expensive consultations and tests and time after time some pompous, greedy, ignorant 'medical rogue' has said to me, 'actually there's nothing wrong with you your tests are normal Mr. Hardy' Followed by, 'have you considered psychiatric help?'

Equally in the NHS I've been abused in far too many situations by 'medical rogues' saying, 'Mr. Hardy there's absolutely nothing wrong with you it's all in your head' and their other favourite line, 'Mr. Hardy we can't keep on testing you why can't you just accept that you have a mental health issue?'

It is primarily because of all the rubbish and abuse I've had to endure that I advocate that we must take control of this situation. How dare some talentless, badly trained yet public sector worker say that the NHS can't keep testing me or anyone of us? I've / we've funded their bloody training, I / we've funded their bloody life styles and some of us have battled to preserve their bloody rotten industry from the ravages of Thatcherism. Boy do those 'charlatans' really make me angry.

My body is the greatest healer of them all and my mind is its engine

You see, I really don't give a hoot if the NHS has to perform a thousand bloody tests upon me to find out what's wrong with me, that's what it's there for and therefore that's what it needs to do. Or it could certainly begin in the name of greater efficiencies, to look at the amount of money it's wasting on fundamentally flawed analytical sciences and clinical investigations and start bring its house in order.

Because if some clerical or 'clinical rogue' is assigning limits to the level of care that I can have from the NHS, then I for one now say let's have voluntary contributions to the NHS. Why should I a potential high earner pay ridiculous amounts of money to underwrite an industry that doesn't want to underwrite me when I need it? Yet it throws billions away on consultant's salaries and treats any chancer who decides to pop over to the UK for treatment.

Now hey I would never in a million years have thought that this working class lad from Woodhouse would ever have held such views towards the NHS. But having been exposed head on to all its woeful underperformance, ignorance and incompetence for years, I'm happy to voice my harsh views now. My belief now is that we need to bring this entire rotten industry crashing to its knees. So that as a nation we're able to build a clinical care service sector that is thorough, competitive; inspirational and world class and let's ditch the clap trap and rubbish of the past.

I now know; who I am, what I am and what I can do, for I am now pain free

The problem with that vision is that the people who have suffered most from its shoddy service are unfortunately the ones with the lowest vitality, presence or voice. So before any of its victims can commit to campaigning for change they need to get well for only then can they hope to bring about change. But be under no illusion that dynamic changes quickly at the point our health returns. Unfortunately the road to recovery can be lonely, long and unrewarding at times and so until we reach our desired destination, its best for all chronically ill patients to focus solely upon regaining their health and leave the clinical reform campaign to better times.

Prior to our return to health however, let me give you a flavour of what happens in the normal psyche when we're experiencing a health condition and require analytical sciences and/or clinical investigations. We immediately make either a big or small deal of the fact that our condition is going to be subject to further scrutiny. Some of us may be worried that something dreadful may be found, whilst others may simply be happy if something could be found to enable us to be treated, recover and move on. I've always come from the school of thought, 'I hope they can find something so that I could move on'. I've never subscribed to worrying about there being something dreadfully wrong with me, because I only ever wanted solutions. I knew for years that I had something seriously wrong with me; I just didn't know what it was. If we don't know what's wrong with us then we can't ever hope to recover and in poor health, recovery must be our sole interest if we wish to regain some form of quality of life. Therefore we must commit to testing and analytical investigations and when the results come through, we must do our level best to acknowledge them and deal with them as appropriately as we're able to or at the very least, see fit.

My body is the greatest healer of them all and my mind is its engine

So let's play the cycle through now, our test results come back and they're always in the standard form of:

- (a) Your tests are normal.
- (b) Hmmn, there is a slight problem but that might just be congenital.
- (c) You have bla bla bla bla.
- (d) You need to make an appointment to discuss your results.

Now to understand the ramifications of that feedback we need to look at the two generic psyches I discussed earlier i.e. big or small deal propensity. So let's look at the big deal psyche first:

(a) Results normal = maybe happy deep down and prepared to take whatever the medical representative says in terms of treatments etc., but may ham it up a bit when speaking to colleagues, family and friends.

(b) Result might be a congenital issue = may be worried deep down yet prepared to take whatever the medical representative says in terms of treatments etc. Might however blow the condition completely out of proportion and will certainly ham it up a bit when speaking to colleagues, family and friends.

(c) Result you have bla bla = may be extremely worried and also might blow the condition completely out of proportion until reassured by the medic, but will certainly ham it up a lot when speaking to colleagues, family and friends.

I now know; who I am, what I am and what I can do, for I am now pain free

(d) Result you need a follow up appointment = extremely worried and will blow the condition completely out of proportion, because that brings the drama they crave into their life. As long as it's a safe and controllable drama that's fine, should it however not be a safe drama then they will start off being publicly very brave and then simply implode putting tremendous pressure on anyone in close proximity.

So let's look at the small deal psyche now:

(a) Results normal = maybe confused deep down but prepared to take to some extent whatever the medical representative says.

(b) Result might be a congenital issue = may be worried but certainly interested in the result more from a clinical perspective than a sensationalist perspective.

(c) Result you have bla bla = may be worried but happy that there is something to discuss, but will need answers.

(d) Result you need a follow up appointment = worried until they understand what's wrong with them, but once they know they just get their heads down with it and are normally stronger than the people around them, who sometimes fall to pieces.

I now know; who I am, what I am and what I can do, for I am now pain free

Now look it doesn't really matter what personality type you fall into. The key to returning to optimum health is ensuring that you're either prepared to be driven or you're prepared to drive the situation. Either way your focus must be upon achieving optimum health, because if you're not experiencing optimum health then you need to understand why; assuming that is that optimum health is your real goal. I've postulated that we must all examine if optimum health is our real goal, and I raise that challenging point because whilst some people will say optimum health is their goal. You only have to talk or listen to them to understand that they are indeed lost or closed to the potential of optimum health. That is because some people really do like being ill, because in being ill they:

- Have the crutch they need.

- Don't need to compete.

- Can offload all their personal issues at the door of their illness or disease.

My body is the greatest healer of them all and my mind is its engine

Now there is absolutely no crime in that, save to say, if a man does not wish to help himself, then perhaps help is not what he needs. You see there are no secrets to optimum health save for a desire to have optimum health, yet within that expectation and desire there are many levels of acceptance and abstinence. Only we as individuals have the sole right to make the value judgments that best meet our desires and needs.

My personal expectations have always been to secure a quality of life that is free from physical impediments and diseased states. Because of that I've mapped a holistic yet pragmatic approach to this process on the next page, now whilst it may initially look complex when you first see it. Just take time to follow some of the evolution and iteration loops from your own perspective and you'll find that it caters precisely for whichever mind set you are.

I now know; who I am, what I am and what I can do, for I am now pain free

Raphael's Treatment Protocol

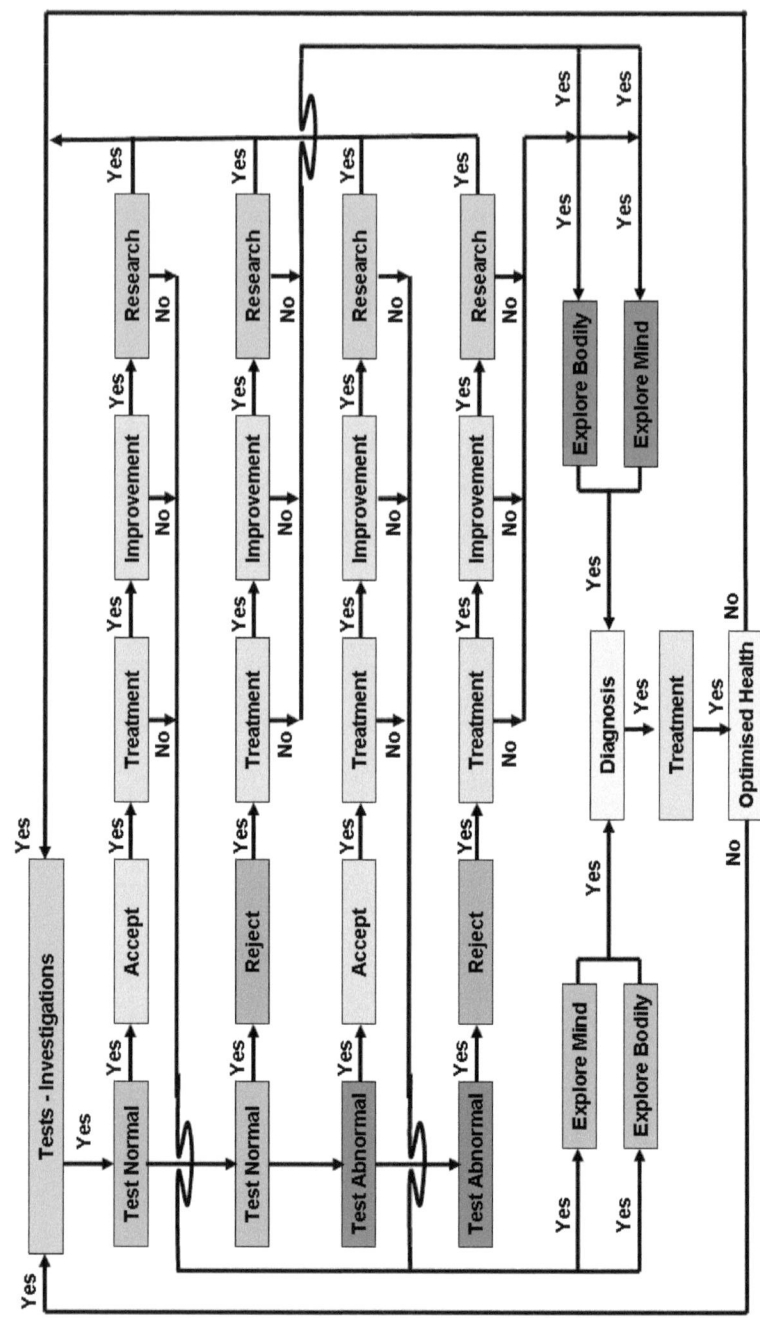

My body is the greatest healer of them all and my mind is its engine

During my pre-diagnostic state my only abstinences were to reject wholesale any and all forms of clap trap or ignorantly manufactured dogma articulated to distract me from my goal. I advocate only this that in the pursuit of optimum health we all must accept that we alone are the responsible party for driving the process of recovery through diagnosis. For without our input, there is no other form of input worthy of comment and therefore no reasonable probability of making any form of sustainable recovery.

Yet whilst that is, or can be, a very difficult path for some of us to walk alone, in reality it's the only path that delivers access to clarity, understanding, effective treatment and recovery. It is by default however; a process of two stages, the first stage is the stage where we are in essence ignorant and unable to make progress because we rely completely upon false testing, consultations and investigations which have little if any merit. I've mapped that process for you on the next page, because once we understand all the loops in the process, it is no longer a mystery and can indeed become that defining point from which we all move forward.

I now know; who I am, what I am and what I can do, for I am now pain free

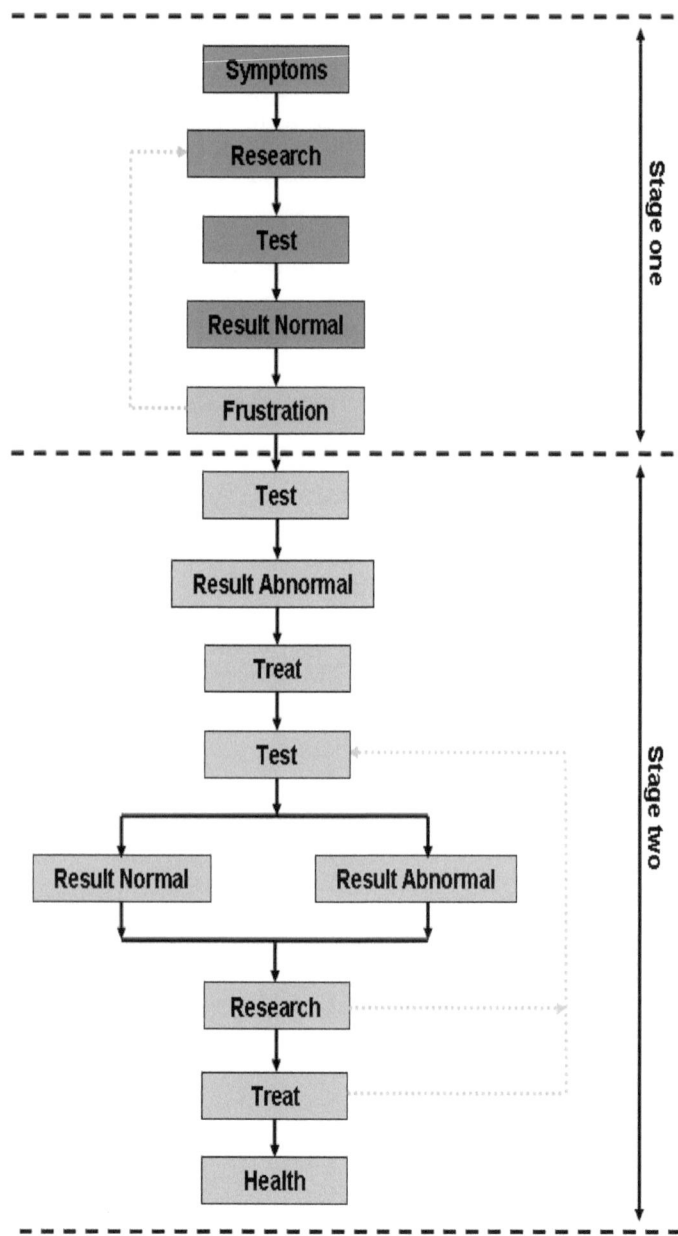

Ignore the doubters who say you can't keep on testing you can and you must

My body is the greatest healer of them all and my mind is its engine

The second stage is where we take ownership of the intellect responsibility for substantiating our underlying condition or conditions. It is the point that we start unravelling our health mysteries, that remarkable point where we see the medical industry and those who support it for what and who they really are.

Both stages are incredibly difficult because they are both encountered when we have lower than normal vitality. Stage one will invariably consist of a 90% - 10% NHS and private involvement whereas 'stage two' will be the complete opposite i.e. 10% - 90% NHS and private involvement.

Therefore there are significant cost implications required of those attempting to return to a position of optimum health. Some of that money will be wasted and some of it will be money well spent. There is no right or wrong course of action to take, all we can ever be is true to ourselves and whilst we can't beat the obscene and perverse nature of the medical industry. We can get better through our own efforts and eventually realise our dreams if only we're prepared to drive the testing and analysis until a reflective diagnosis has been achieved. In my particular situation stage one of my investigation process consisted of nothing more than the following fundamentally flawed investigations below:

- 3 Liver enzyme tests.

- 3 Thyroid tests.

- 1 MRI.

- 1 CT.

- 1 X-ray investigation.

I now know; who I am, what I am and what I can do, for I am now pain free

The conclusions drawn from them were that I was fine and had nothing wrong with me except for mental health issues, time and time again. Whereas my stage two self funded investigations included:

- 5 MRI's.
- 2 MRA's.
- 4 CAT scans.
- 2 CT's.
- 60+ blood tests and bodily function analysis, tests and examinations.
- 9 Caloric Tests.
- 3 Hearing Tests.
- 9 ENG Tests.
- Two Neurosurgical procedures.
- 180+ clinical consultations all around the world plus travel and accommodation.
- Plus thousands of hours research on the internet long before cheap broad band, etc.
- In summation personal traceable costs in excess of 300K.

The result of my tenacity in the face of unbelievable odds was that I was eventually diagnosed with:

- Chronic late stage Lymes Disease.

- Chronic mitochondria failure.

- Chronic liver disease.

- Chronic adrenal insufficiency.

- And an extremely rare genetic yet organic anomaly resulting in a Posterior Inferior Cerebella Artery insulting my vestibular bundle and brain stem left side. *Note this condition still imposes great suffering upon me every minute of every day and that's why just putting my thoughts onto paper is such an almighty affair.*

Now look, the point I'm making is that there are far too many issues surrounding our poor medical investigation model and too many issues surrounding outdated machines and devices being postulated as state of the art diagnostic tools. How many of us actually know until we are faced with horrendous medical conditions just how bad the equipment and techniques used to analyse our bodies truly are through-out the nhs because if we did I'm sure our own dogs of war would be unleashed.

I now know; who I am, what I am and what I can do, for I am now pain free

How many of us have been for an MRI scan and been told that everything is normal, when in reality the MRI scanner being used is:

- Badly designed and maintained?

- Outdated and malfunctioning?

- An expensive piece of scrap metal?

- Operated by people who don't give a shit.

Now we all know the difference between top and low end motoring in terms of performance etc, but very few of us know that the same is the case in the medical industry. You see, in the push to kid us all into thinking our health is safe in their hands, NHS trusts all around the country installed sub standard equipment which in the majority of instances are nothing more than token gestures in terms of world class clinical investigation tools. The differences are so wide in terms of performing basic functions that it's like giving one man a set of binoculars and another an electron microscope to analyse the same bacteria, now that would be simply ridiculous wouldn't it?

Well the truth is, the state of our nation's clinical diagnostic tools is not simply ridiculous, it's actually a disgrace and we the front end users or mugs are the ones paying the highest price. We're sent for diagnostic investigations, the results come back normal and the result of that is, no further line of investigation undertaken despite the fact that your condition may continue to decline.

My body is the greatest healer of them all and my mind is its engine

Simply because a shit piece of equipment operated by people who don't give a shit has indicating that you have no problem or in point of fact is unable to detect the problem you have. Now I sincerely hope that my observations through suffering and personal wasted expense has set off some alarm bells deep within you because those alarm bells need to resonate with us all as a society each and every day because we need this resolved not next year or next month I would respectfully suggest but tomorrow and it must happen before lunch time at the very latest.

Because I advocate that when and where there is evidence to suggest that the instruments, techniques, systems and protocols used to support clinical investigations are incapable of investigating with the degree of enquiry that we need, then we need to:

- Challenge the results.

- Find suitable systems etc, which can perform to the level and standard of integrity that we require.

You see, I'm no solo foot soldier here, millions of us are being written off every year by fundamentally flawed medical investigations, consultations and tests. So if you truly desire optimum health, you're going to have to fight for it with all your intellect, strength and might. You're going to have to:

- Ignore the personal and clinical prejudices that you encounter.

- You're going to have to spend money that you may not have.

- You're going to have to prove your condition yourself.

I now know; who I am, what I am and what I can do, for I am now pain free

Because if you think for one moment that the state, the NHS or our private medical health circus will resolve anything more than a superficial health impediment then your sadly mistaken because they won't. Only you can drive this stage two part of your pursuit of disease expression reflective diagnosis, because in reality there really only is you who truly gives a damn. So to help keep you upbeat and focused during that process I've mapped a very simple process approach plan for you below.

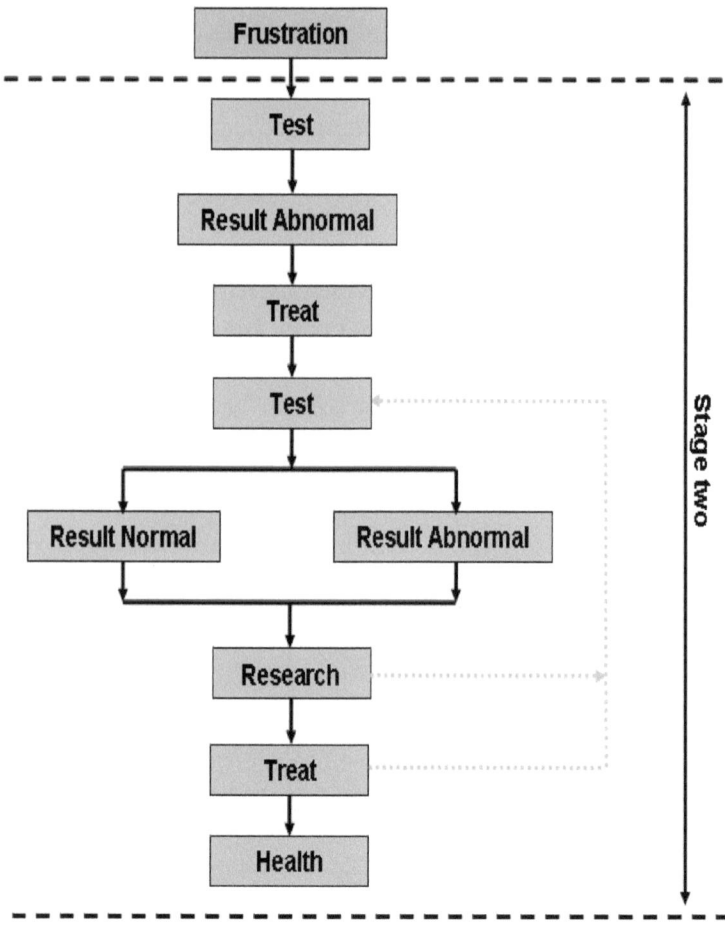

Ignore the doubters who say you can't keep on testing you can and you must

My body is the greatest healer of them all and my mind is its engine

So that when you're at the other end of your health recovery campaign you can then speak from a platform of assurance, confidence and righteousness. You can challenge the integrity of those who failed you, ignored or abused you, because at that point you're more than an equal for anyone who would choose to play games with you because you're able to ask with assurance:

- Why are we as a nation wasting so much money on fundamentally flawed tests etc., whilst writing people off with impunity?

- Why are some of us, with a desire to be well, having to self research, self fund and self acquire best in class medical and clinical investigations outside the UK?

- Where is the medical establishment when we need it?

- Who within our current appalling medical service sector ranks can dare to defend this level of clinical and administrated incompetence?

I now know; who I am, what I am and what I can do, for I am now pain free

Raphael's Treatment Protocol

There really is only one way to ensure that you get through your health predicaments and that is to take control of your stage two process whilst ensuring you stay in total control of your entire health optimisation process re: below.

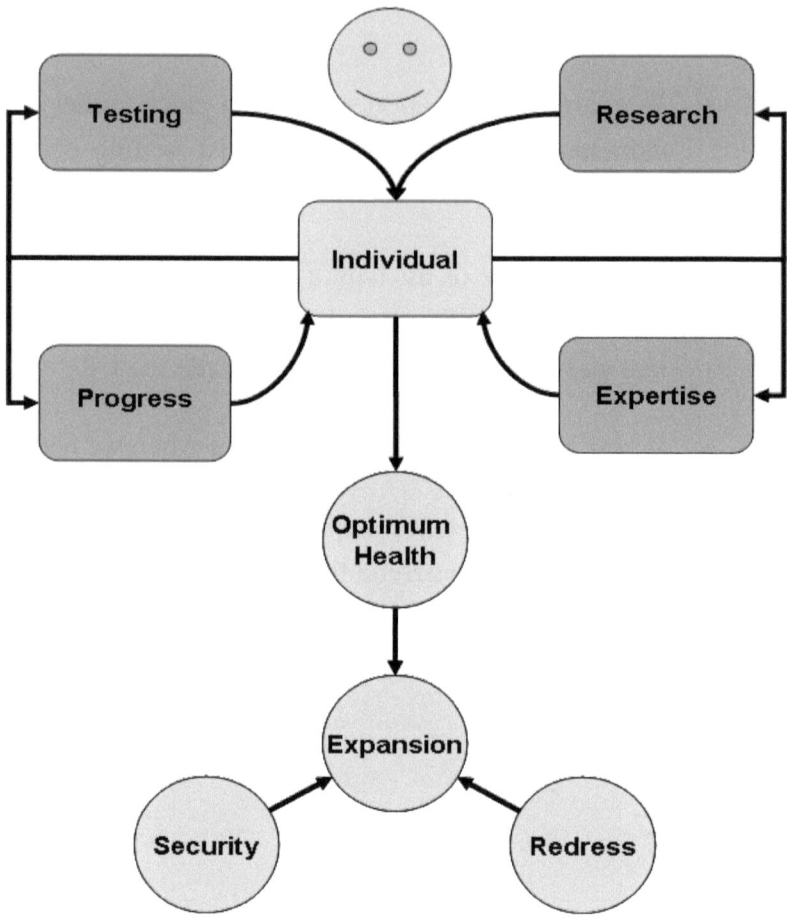

Taking Individual Control of All Health Related Processes

My body is the greatest healer of them all and my mind is its engine

Personal Notes

I now know; who I am, what I am and what I can do, for I am now pain free

Personal Notes

My body is the greatest healer of them all and my mind is its engine

EXPLORING ANALYTICAL TESTING OPTIONS PRAGMATICALLY

Exploration Seven

I now know; who I am, what I am and what I can do, for I am now pain free

My body is the greatest healer of them all and my mind is its engine

I've made great play throughout this book of the need for effective testing and re-testing if necessary, to enable effective diagnosis of underlying diseased states. Yet whilst those tests can take many forms including: imaging and bodywork. I believe that the key to identifying the root cause of any chronic condition begins with effective blood and biochemical marker analysis. The clinic that I used for my detailed blood analysis via my private GP Dr. Sarah Myhill referrals was 'Biolab Medical Unit UK'.

Biolab Medical Unit is a; medical referral laboratory specializing in nutritional and environmental medicine which is located in the heart of the West End of London. They are a nutritional biochemistry laboratory measuring vitamin and mineral levels, toxic metals, other biochemical levels that are related to the availability of vitamins, minerals and other nutrients. They have an extensive range of profiles for assessing the effects of twenty-first century lifestyles on our bodies and are dedicated to assisting doctor's sort out their patients' problems in a way that does not rely on drugs as a first line of treatment. Biolab apply modern scientific laboratory analytical methods to establish what imbalances there are in the bodies of those who are suffering ill-health or non-optimum health, so that these imbalances may be addressed via nutritional and non-drug means, with the aim of achieving good health or, at least, improving the quality of life and minimizing suffering.

I would therefore suggest that it's worth visiting their website at www.biolab.co.uk/ for a more detailed overview of their services, staff and publications etc. However please note that Biolab Medical Unit (UK) is a referral unit and will only perform tests requested by practitioners registered with;

- The General Medical Council.

I now know; who I am, what I am and what I can do, for I am now pain free

- The General Dental Council.

- The General Osteopathic Council.

- The General Chiropractic Council.

All test reports will be sent to your practitioner as Biolab will not enter into direct discussions with you about your results, although they are happy to discuss their findings in relation to your tests with your practitioner. It's important to note that I have absolutely no commercial, professional or personal arrangement with Biolab Medical Unit or any other analytical service provider. Furthermore those services providers will be completely unaware of my personal use of their services or my recommendation of their services. I would nevertheless strongly urge any individual suffering from a chronic health condition and wishing to undergo private blood investigations etc., to discuss their case with their medical/clinical service provider and request that they enter into discussions with respective analytical service providers such as Biolab. But be under no illusion that you may find that an uphill battle because medics in general traditionally poo poo anything that deviates from their own ignorant perspectives. If that is the outcome of your discussions then you have only three choices open to you:

(a) Stay with your current service provider.

(b) Secure more appropriate service support.

Or

My body is the greatest healer of them all and my mind is its engine

(c) Give up completely on life.

Ultimately as the masters of our own health and happiness we must make the choices we feel are best for us and in that we must be prepared to stand or fall, live or die by the choices we choose to make.

I now know; who I am, what I am and what I can do, for I am now pain free

My body is the greatest healer of them all and my mind is its engine

EXPLORING RAPHAEL'S TREATMENT PROTOCOL PRAGMATICALLY

Exploration Eight

I now know; who I am, what I am and what I can do, for I am now pain free

My body is the greatest healer of them all and my mind is its engine

Now then; there's been a lot of words, a lot of postulations and lot of my prejudicial views in this book thus far. But I'm not naive enough to think that anyone reading this book will fully understand and feel completely at ease with the points that I've been making about my alternative approach to chronic illness expression eradication. Nevertheless if some of what I've had to say has stimulated your thought processes about your current and/or past chronic illness expressions, then I've managed at least to realise one of my main initial objectives. You see; I believe that when we begin to explore well trodden boundaries within our lives and psyche that we've previously considered as rigid constraints. We're frequently rewarded either directly or indirectly with completely different and rewarding insights about things that we've either taken for granted and/or written off has having no overall validity. That being said I'm now going to cover in the final few pages of this book a simple approach to chronic illness detection that may challenge your perceptions of your current or past chronic illness expressions to their core. The key as ever to my postulations of securing better health is personal ownership and sensibility to your overall wellbeing and under no circumstance putting yourself at any significant risk. You see; no one should have to live with irresolvable chronic illness expression, because it is neither a karmic lesson nor an opportunity to grow, but that doesn't mean to say we should take risks in our attempts to recover for the same because in doing so there is always the potential of making our situation much much worse.

I now know; who I am, what I am and what I can do, for I am now pain free

Poor quality of life and health are nothing more than blights upon our lives and so no matter which way anyone chooses to look at it. The expression of unresolved chronic illness expression in society at large needs to be removed from our society and psyche completely right now. Not tomorrow, not next week or next month or next year, but today, this minute, right now. Because despite what anyone ever says to you about the seemingly irresolvable nature of your illness, you can get better if you draw upon all the skills and intellect at your disposal and commit to an holistic program of physical well being though disease originator eradication.

We all deserve good health and what's more we have a right to it and that's not open to question, but the word on the street and the word that I'm proclaiming loud and clear is; 'CAUTION' at all times, because without that there is always the real possibility of antagonizing your already fragile well being capabilities. If we wish to recover from chronic ill health we must take our health seriously and under no circumstance undertake any investigation or treatment activity without suitable supervision and/or medical/clinical guidance. When we commit to an educated and scientific regime of testing, investigation, qualification and treatment, we're actually providing our body and our resolve with all that they need to bring about a state of physical wellbeing, Amen.

My body is the greatest healer of them all and my mind is its engine

A CASE FOR PERSONAL EXPLORATION

There is one sure fire thing about anyone suffering from chronic illness expression and that is; suffers will do and take anything they can to remove it from their life. The majority in the end resort to escapist options because living in their body is simply beyond mortal endurance and the options include:

- Exercise.
- Deviant acts.
- Drugs.
- Cigarettes.
- Alcohol.
- Orthodox medication.
- Herbal supplements.
- Homeopathy.

And even

- Suicide attempts.

Whilst others commit to

- Suicide completions.

Such is the suffering of those, experiencing unrelenting, chronic, chronic illness expression that for most their only constant thought is that of finding somehow or some way of detaching themselves from its grasp. I know only too well the depth of that despair for there is not a treatment, a medication, a supplement, an activity or self destruct approach that I have not committed to over a thirty year period of suffering.

I now know; who I am, what I am and what I can do, for I am now pain free

Simply because no matter who I sort help from, which treatment I undertook, NOTHING and I mean NOTHING removed chronic illness expression from my life until I solved the problem through root cause analysis myself. For over thirty years I was medically and clinically abused, mistreated, misdiagnosed and blamed for all my presenting symptoms. In the end the only thing open to me was a state imposed psychiatric incarceration, which I somehow managed to negate, but that I'm afraid is the only option open to far too many desperate souls. However I'm stating firmly for the record that it's possible to lower chronic illness expression rapidly. In fact it's possible to feel better than you've ever felt in your life before. Yet my approach doesn't include either;

- Self beasting through Psychoanalysis.

Or

- Detachment though 'Somnolence' inducing concoctions.

Or

- A combination of both ridiculous approaches.

My body is the greatest healer of them all and my mind is its engine

My Raphael Treatment Protocol (RTP) consists of nothing more than:

1. Introduction
2. Testing requirements.
3. Root cause analysis and iterative review.
4. Control agents' qualification.
5. Cellular cleansing agents.

And

6. Summary cost analysis.

All undertaken in the understanding that:

1. You must have access to and be supervised by a suitably qualified practitioner.
2. You must NOT stop any treatment protocol you're currently undertaking until your blood and fats analysis results have been compiled and a supervised way forward has been agreed.

INTRODUCTION

The Raphael Treatment Protocol (RTP) is all about moving forward quickly from a point of chronic illness and points of isolation, suffering and pain but leaving that place in a state of clarity. The RTP is unlike any other healing process you've ever encountered because its whole body focused via scientific analysis. A series of steps that removes anecdotal subjectivity from your healing process, because your foundation for moving forward is based upon the analysis of scientific FACT in relation to your whole being. That combined with greater scientific understanding of disease generation and propagation resulting from the insights generated in all of my self help books *'which you should have read by now'*. In having access to those materials you should understand by now that there is a need to self fund a whole range of specialist tests to ensure that your underlying disease can be qualified.

Note that you cannot begin to move forward into your recovery if you're not prepared to subject yourself to effective scientific analysis and so that is something you must come to terms with quickly.

My body is the greatest healer of them all and my mind is its engine

Raphael's Treatment Protocol

TESTING REQUIREMENTS

As a starting point in your recovery you must be prepared to accept that you will have to pay for several highly specialised blood and bodily function tests made up of four stages

Stage One

    i. Mitochondria Analysis.
    ii. Methylation Process Analysis.
    iii. Sulphanation Process Analysis.
    iv. Whole Body Toxin Analysis
    v. Whole Body Mineral Analysis.
    vi. Whole Body Enzyme Analysis.

Stage one testing of the RTP testing process is all about understanding how well your body is functioning in terms of detoxing your body of the toxins and the debris generated from disease impositions.

Stage Two

    vii. Lymes Disease Analysis.
    viii. Chlamydia Analysis.
    ix. Herpes Disease Analysis.
    x. Bronchitis Analysis.
    xi. Syphilis Analysis.
    xii. Viral Analysis.
    xiii. Sand Fly Disease Analysis.
    xiv. Candida Disease Analysis.
    xv. Fungal Analysis.

I now know; who I am, what I am and what I can do, for I am now pain free

Stage two testing of the RTP testing process is all about understanding which diseases and or combinations of diseases are imposing a diseased state upon your whole body state of wellness.

Stage Three

> xvi. Thyroid Analysis.
>
> xvii. A 24 hour Saliva Adrenal Function test.

Stage three testing of the RTP testing process is all about understanding how well your endocrine system is functioning and what impact disease is having upon your body's ability to support your whole body state of wellness.

Stage Four

> xviii. Lipo Bio / Nuro Toxin Analysis

Stage four testing of the RTP testing process is all about understanding how toxic your body is and what impact that toxic load is having upon your body's ability to support your whole body state of wellness.

ROOT CAUSE ANALYSIS AND ITERATIVE REVIEW

There is only one way to recover from chronic illness and that is to analyse the results of all mandatory yet staged analytical blood tests, therein; compiling a clear picture re: the process mapping tool below. Without that you're unable to qualify a suitable treatment protocol.

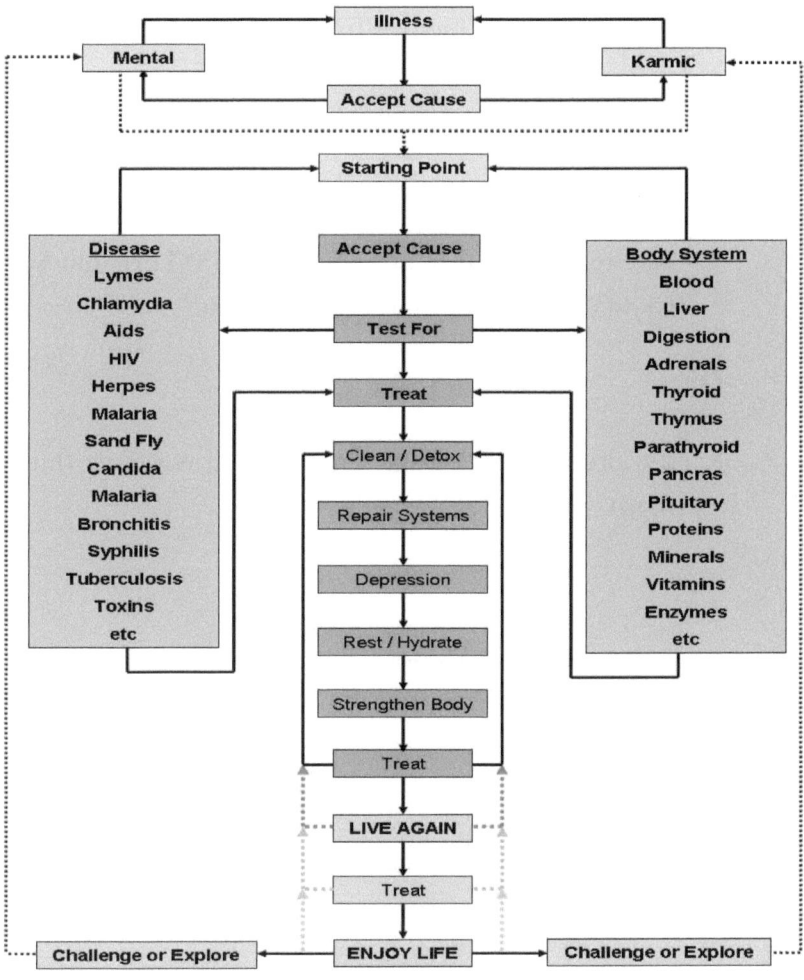

I now know; who I am, what I am and what I can do, for I am now pain free

CONTROL AGENTS' QUALIFICATION

Once you have qualified which disease state impositions are directly and / or indirectly adversely affecting your whole body, you can then decide if you wish to go down the:

- Orthodox medication routes.
- Herbal / natural medication routes
- Homeopathic medication routes.

However my preferred options are;

- One tea spoon of Higher Nature 'MSM organic Sulphur Crystals' in water morning and night.

Or

- 2-5 drops NutraMedix 'Samento' in water morning and night.

Or

- 2-5 drops NutraMedix 'Cumanda' in water morning and night.

Or

- 2-5 drops Higher Nature 'Citricidal' Grapefruit Seed Liquid Extract in water morning and night.

Or

- Rife Machine technology once per week.

Or

- I table spoon of 'Himalayan Rock Salt Soley' morning and night.

It should be noted that I have absolutely no commercial or clinical / medical arrangement with either Higher Nature or NutraMedix including any other directly or indirectly associated party. I'm merely citing their products simply because I found them to work well for me. These are natural yet highly potent products which can be bought online or from any good health food store. These products are antimicrobial, antibacterial and anti-inflammatory which mean's that they will immediately kill foreign invaders whilst reducing initially some of any directly or indirectly associated inflammation. The result of that action in individuals suffering from chronic illness is that they will immediately experience:

1. Changes in mode i.e. their mood will be lifted immediately and may even move slightly into a hyper or manic mode.

And

2. Any associated pain that the sufferer may be use to, will be significantly reduced or removed completely.

Before

3. The sufferer's mood will be drastically lowered again and all associated pain will increase with additional pain being generated in new and strange locations.

I now know; who I am, what I am and what I can do, for I am now pain free

Now the reason all that happens time after time is because that is the standard Herxheimer Reaction (HR) that people with chronic disease states incur at the point they begin to address their diseased state. It's a toxic reaction generated in the body by toxins being released from dead or decaying parasites, fungus, viruses, bacteria and / or other pathogens. As these toxins circulate in our body, it is not uncommon to experience flu-like symptoms including headache, joint and muscle pain, body aches, sore throat, general malaise, sweating, chills, nausea or other symptoms. This is a normal and indicates that parasites, fungus, viruses, bacteria or other pathogens are being effectively killed off. The biggest battle we all face in recovering from chronic illness expression is dealing with the HR in a way that enables us to function and ensure that we can continue to medicate and support our bodies through what is a truly hellish situation. I myself have arrived at that point now because after years of self treating and suffering I've found the formula that allows me to kill my bodily invaders whilst supporting my defective detox capabilities via a number of gentle treatment protocols not least of which includes the use of a far infrared sauna daily. But I will cover that in the very next section i.e. Cellular Cleansing Agents, but before I do that here is one important point I need to make here in relation to the support of the endocrine system. That is that I completely agree with the medication of small doses of hormones in terms of:

1. Hydrocortisol and / or prednisolone to support the adrenals, *which can be purchased online without a prescription.*

And

2. Synthetic Armour to support the thyroid, *which can be purchased online without a prescription.*

So whilst pompous medics will cry foul on that matter and cite my support of such medications as evidence of my cavalier and ludicrous approach wellness. All I can say is that in controlled and supervised dosage both medication offer far greater positives than negatives and in fact are probably less dangerous when handled with integrity than:

- Alcohol.

- Cigarettes.

- High fat foods.

- Controlled substances such as:

    I. Crack cocaine.

    II. Heroine.

    III. Marijuana etc.

All off which whilst covered by government health warnings and criminality policy etc, can be consumed in a completely irresponsibly fashion. But all are unfortunately addictive and damage many things not least of which includes; Gaba receptors and associated neuro-networks leading to emotional/psychological complications. Such is the addictive nature of some of those substances when used indiscriminately by individuals with chronic stress and depression expression as a means

I now know; who I am, what I am and what I can do, for I am now pain free

of acquiring momentary release, that they often find themselves eventually either in prison or on enforced psychiatric retention. Now that's not really what I would call the acts of responsible individuals and it is therefore in no way associated with the responsible use of endocrine support supplements that I personally advocate. You see; I'm an ardent supporter of controlled endocrine system support where there is good cause to do so, because I personally believe that if we exclude illegal substance abuse, I would nevertheless respectfully suggest that there are far too many so called clinically supervised individuals pumping far too much so called orthodox toxins into their bodies including:

- Prescription medication in the form of SSRI's etc.

With the majority of them making absolutely no progress in their desperate attempts to acquire some resolution from their chronic stress and depression expressions but who have somehow fallen into the deadly medical/clinical:

- Psychiatric treatment trap, with all is shortfalls and associated medical/clinical abuse loops.

And

- Compromising their body's recovery processes further via the highly toxic effects of such medications upon their methylation and sulphanation processes which are desperately needed to function effectively if one is to assume a reasonable state of well-being free from chronic illness expression.

My body is the greatest healer of them all and my mind is its engine

CELLULAR CLEANSING AGENTS

I have a real problem with the whole subject of blood cleaning and body detoxing because there is so much ignorance and crap out there in terms what constitutes effective approaches and as someone who been through the mill on this subject I'm of the opinion that CAUTION is needed on this front completely. I would therefore urge you to ignore any anecdotal quotes about how effective any given supplement and/or detox regime is in terms of removing toxins etc, from the body. Because frankly, as someone who ingested literally thousands of pounds of products and underwent too many flawed detox treatments over to many years. None of the treatments or supplements that I explored are worthy of any further consideration. The majority of my treatments did little at all to help me and the rest simply pushed me as chronically ill person into a deeper chronic state. Because none of the treatments that I explored even remotely understood defects with and to our methylation and sulphanation processes let alone being in any way remotely sympathetic to the simply desperate state of those suffering from chronic illness. However if you've found something that works for you on this front then stick with it, because I always believe that if it works don't tamper with it, all I say is be very very careful. Nevertheless I will be very clear here, the only things that have ever worked to help me reduce my state of chronic disease expression by helping to remove and/or lower my overall toxic load are:

- My FIR sauna of which I've purchased two in my time a static and mobile version, FIR used 4 times x 1 hour per week.

And

- R-Lipoic Acid which is the stable potassium salt form of Alpha Lipioc Acid.

So please do you own personal research here and attempt to qualify for yourself what you believe will work for you. But again I imploring you not to read too much into anecdotal web based intellectual salmonella about toxic overload eradication, otherwise you may end up making yourself so much worse.

SUMMARY COST ANALYSIS.

It's a fact that chronic ill health imposes upon us all as contributory members of our nation state and as individuals in our own right an excessive cost burden and there's absolutely no getting away from that. The point I would make as a former sufferer of chronic ill health is that I chose to spend my way out of that whether I had the funds at the time or even not, simply because the state which I'd contributed to all my working life simply failed me on all fronts. Furthermore because I know just how little effective support there is out there for people suffering from chronic illness I've concluded over time that:

- We can either accept that we need to self fund our way out of chronic illness and in doing so bypass the inadequacies that underwrite our current state funded medical/clinical model.

Or

- We can stick with our current state funded medical/clinical model and accept that it's both moralistically and ethically acceptable to be written off and forced to suffer forever.

Either way

- Each individual's has the right to make the choice that best meets their aspirations and needs and I would never ever argue with the right of choice.

I now know; who I am, what I am and what I can do, for I am now pain free

Nevertheless

- If you choose to self fund your own route to recovery then its best that you understand some of those costs.

Because I've been through a difficult and exceptionally expensive process, I believe that the pursuit of recovery from chronic illness now comes in at a fraction of what I had to spend. So much so that this is now my cost summary of expense required in support of recovery from chronic ill health in the primary recovery year, albeit accepting that each case will have slightly different requirements.

Supervisory consultation costs	£500.00
Blood analysis tests	£2000.00
Supplements & medications	£400.00
FIR sauna	£350.00
Total	**£3250.00**

Which effectively means a cost of 1% of what it cost me to recover!

My body is the greatest healer of them all and my mind is its engine

SUMMATION

With all process control models there is a requirement for analytical determination followed by both linear progression and iteration where analytical investigations suggest a need to rethink. Therefore I've mapped those two key process models for you to help you through your own RTP and they are figures 1 re: below and figure 2 next page.

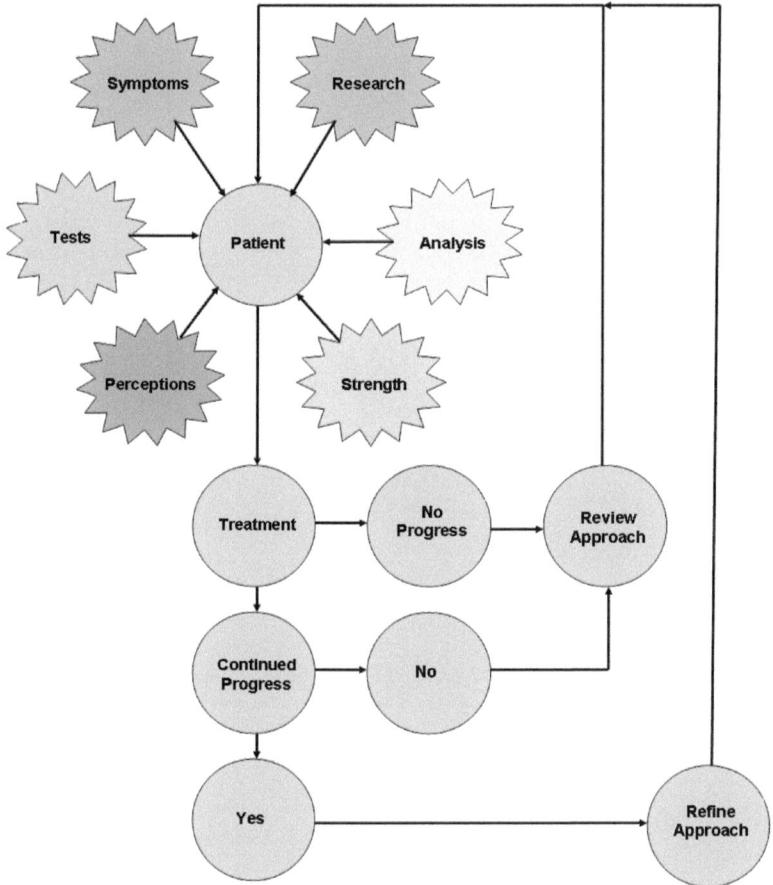

The return of optimum health, requires nothing more than optimum clarity of intent

Figure 1

I now know; who I am, what I am and what I can do, for I am now pain free

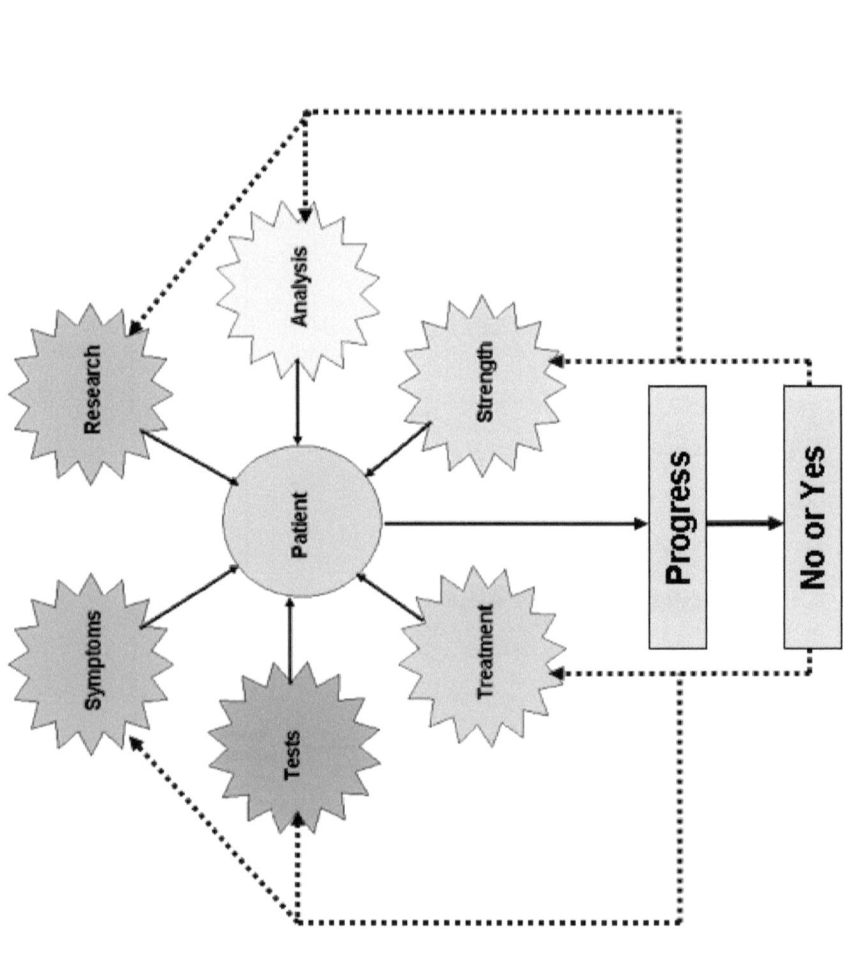

Figure 2

My body is the greatest healer of them all and my mind is its engine

RAPHAEL TREATMENT PROTOCOL RECAP SUMMARY

- You must be prepared to look objectively at your results with your practitioner and understand exactly what is actually happening and/or going on in your body.

- You must be prepared to undertake supervised treatment regimes designed to:

    1. Quash any microorganism disease states.
    2. Support and energize any diseased organ states.
    3. Support your bodies detoxing capabilities.

- Monitor your body at every stage of your treatment protocol re: figures 1 and 2, because it's vitally important to know where you're at during any stage of your recovery and management process.

- Above all be gentle with yourself because the road to recovery is full of ups and downs during the process of disease eradication, toxin removal and whole body system re-energization.

Be under no illusion however, that at the point you begin to address any underlying disease states and instigate effective toxin removal, you will immediately begin to feel better. Thereafter windows of freedom from chronic illness expression will become more frequent until its expression in your life is nothing more than a far distant episode from a horror story that you chose and continue to choose to leave behind.

I now know; who I am, what I am and what I can do, for I am now pain free

The key is to remember that the process of healing can be accelerated when we take control of effective root cause analysis etc, a dynamic clearly profiled in my pictorial healing times lines (a) and (b) and qualifying in (c) and (d) the dynamic of understanding whether you're on the correct treatment rationale for you or not. You see; there are no great rewards for anyone in unnecessary suffering because it adds very little to our life at all. Therefore we must always listen to our body and our higher self and learn to understand the truth and/or substance of everything we hear, read, see or feel in our body as we pursue our quest of a greater and better quality of life. Without that personal commitment, there is no real potential for whole body healing, because the process of healing both begins and ends with our ability to self nurture, self solve and self support our bodies throughout our entire and overall healing process. Because in truth, we're the only ones who can give it our full and highly considered attention and that's because, invariably we're the only ones who truly care.

My body is the greatest healer of them all and my mind is its engine

My Actual Healing Time Line
Time Line (a)

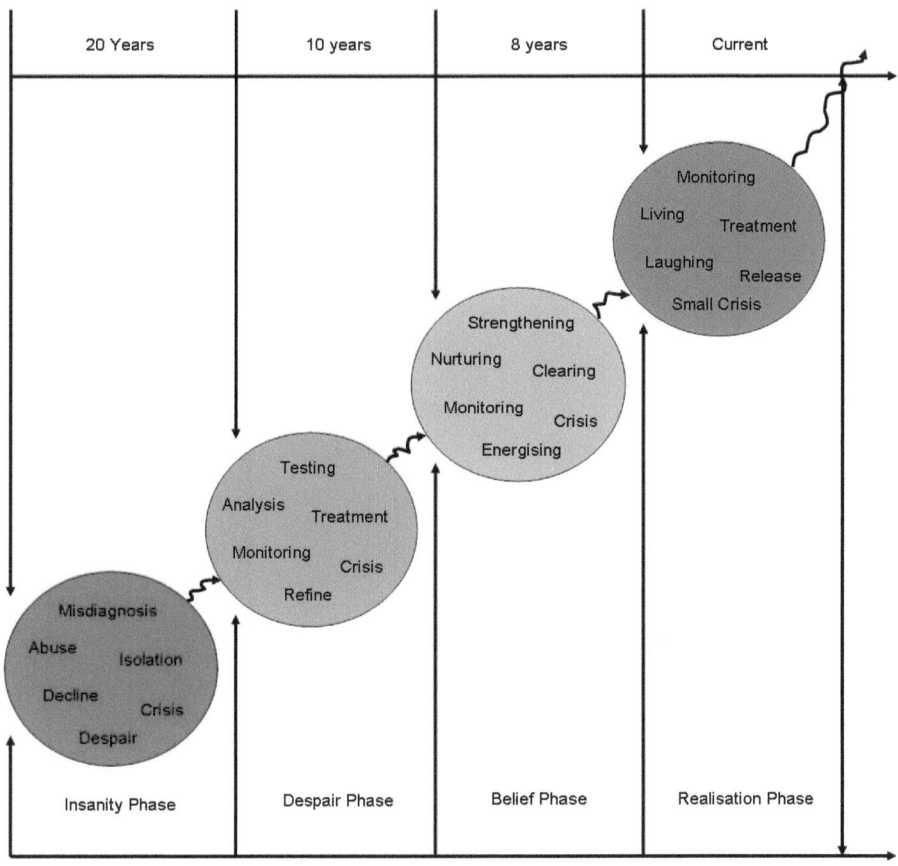

I now know; who I am, what I am and what I can do, for I am now pain free

Possible Healing Time Line 4U
Time Line (b)

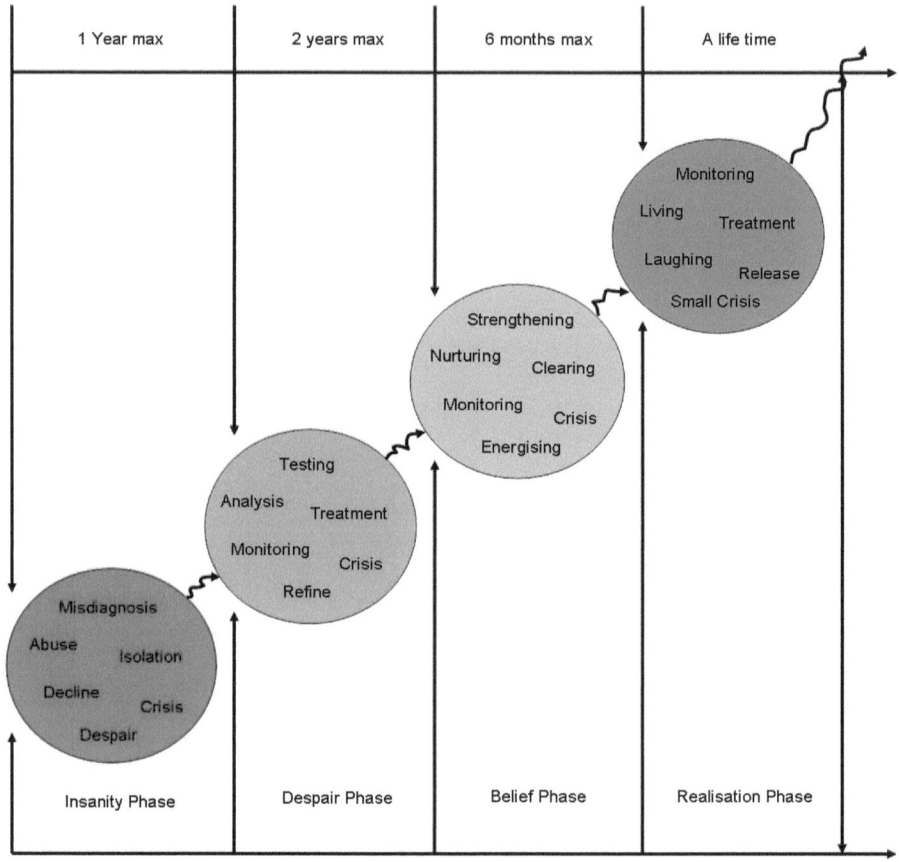

Time is only the great healer when our healing time is spent well

My body is the greatest healer of them all and my mind is its engine

Inappropriate Treatment Time Line 4U
Time Line (c)

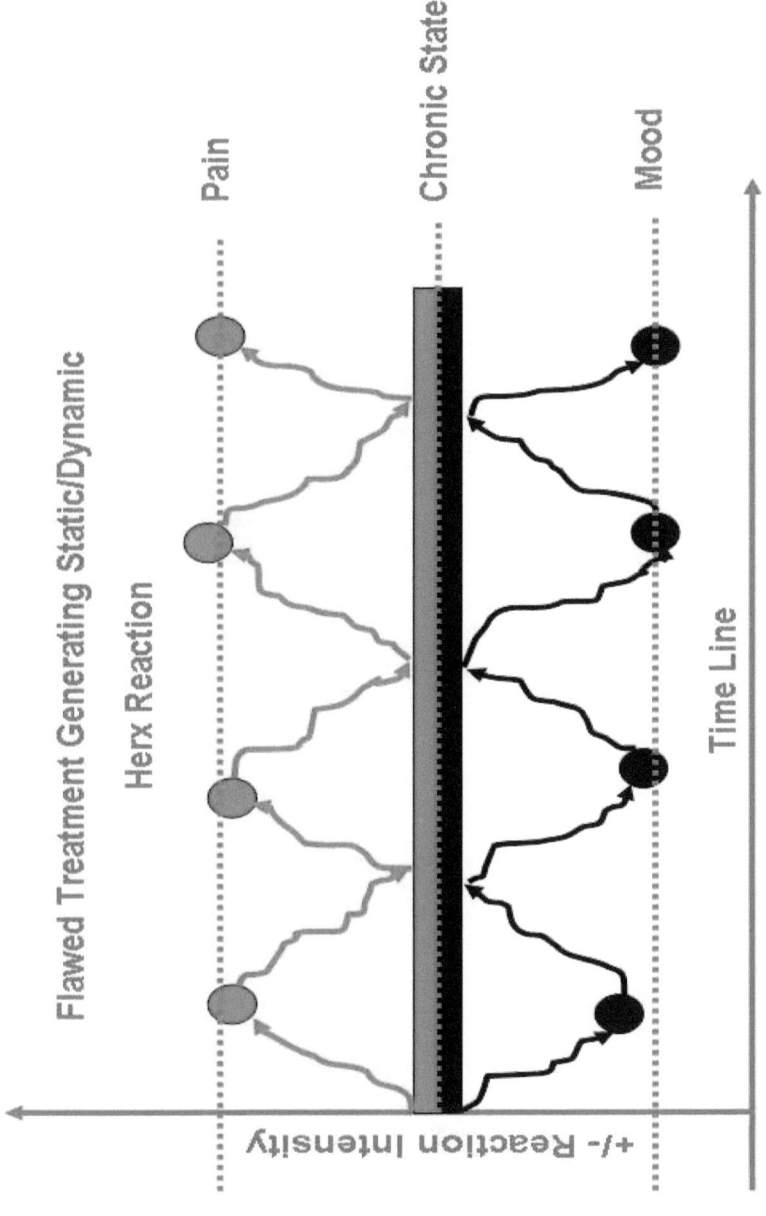

I now know; who I am, what I am and what I can do, for I am now pain free

Correct Treatment Time Line 4U
Time Line (d)

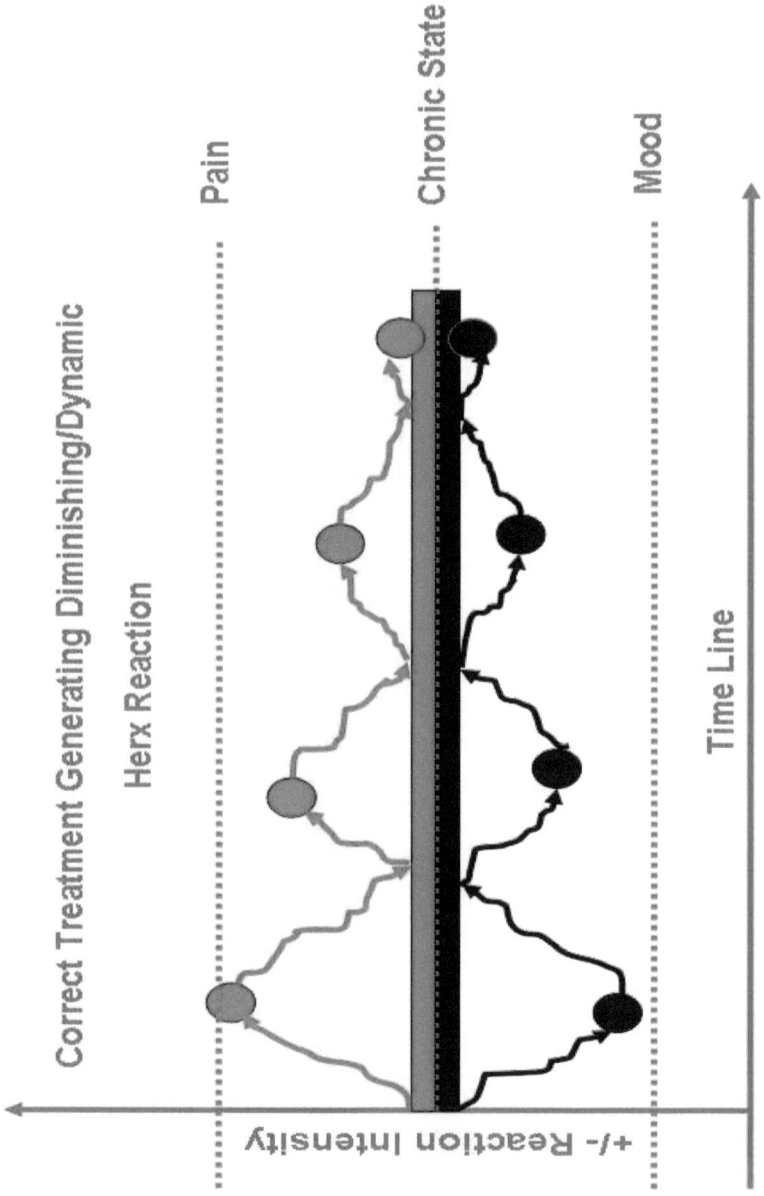

My body is the greatest healer of them all and my mind is its engine

Personal Notes

I now know; who I am, what I am and what I can do, for I am now pain free

Personal Notes

My body is the greatest healer of them all and my mind is its engine

AUTHORS NOTES

I now know; who I am, what I am and what I can do, for I am now pain free

My body is the greatest healer of them all and my mind is its engine

Personal Insight and Ownership

I'm aware that I've scared and troubled many people in the past with my ability to: analyse, condemn, congratulate and even poke fun at myself in the pursuit of reality and my own personal progression. I'm a very big believer that personal insight and personal ownership of all our mortal endeavours is the key to a truly considered life. Therefore if the tone, substance and/or in-depth of personal expression or certain aspects of my personal life are too much for any of my readers. I would respectfully suggest that perhaps its time for them to stop reading and start writing, for the expression of repression certainly offers release as far as I understand, from the tension we all as mortals appear to manufacture with ease.

Medics and the Medical/Clinical World

The medical world is full of humans each with their own unique gifts, skills and personal flaws and it's because the medical world is full of mortals and not earth God's that they fail us so badly day after day. But don't just sit back any longer when you're abused, let down or failed by anyone in the medical/clinical world. Sue them and bring them and their industry to account if you desire, for in doing so you will not only help yourself via the pursuit of redress, but indirectly you'll play a very big part in helping the entire human race.

I now know; who I am, what I am and what I can do, for I am now pain free

The Great Psychological Bluff and Scandal

If we allow others to cloud our realities in terms of who we are and what we're actually experiencing with inappropriate postulations about the state of our psychology, be under no illusion we fail ourselves completely at every conceivable level. On matters of psychology when pursuing well-being, listen to your antagonists but choose not to hear when you're being written as another psychological basket case. Because I'm confident you'll discover if you test your body thoroughly, that it's your body that's at fault not your emotions or mind. At that point all psychological assertions can be met head on as you pursue a meaningful life.

Eminently Solvable Conditions

When you're health conditions are being fudged and written off as illnesses that have only names with no treatment or resolution options open or offered to you to help you get by or simply cope. You really have only two options open to you and that is to stick with what you've got if that's all you can do or you can test and test until your condition or conditions are identified. We are all the sole guardians of our own mortality; therefore we can either relinquish our responsibility to the uncaring and obscene or we can fight for what is our mortal right, the right to decency and an acceptable quality of life.

My body is the greatest healer of them all and my mind is its engine

Depression Expression

There is no insanity at all in depression expression save only for the sheer depth of suffering its victims incur. Because the reality is that depression expression can be eradicated in days, not weeks, months or years when the physical generators, precursors and accelerators of depression expression are treated and removed. All that is needed is a shift in perceptions, a position significantly enhanced by holistic treatment results.

Stressful Resolution

Whilst the majority of us have experienced some degree of stress at some point in our life, very few of us realise that it's so predictable, so treatable and so recoverable from, hence nothing whatsoever for us all to get stressed about. Once you understand the dynamics, your stress levels will fall and at that point you will wonder why you allowed yourself to get so stressed in the first place or indeed at all.

Wellness

There is no great secret to wellness over and above understanding the root cause of any decline from wellness into un-wellness. But that root-cause analysis is not determined by non intrusive subjective analysis, because it can only be determined by holistic, scientific testing and analysis. Anything less than that is mere supposition, supposition however has never cured anyone or created a state of considered wellbeing, but it has forced many poor mortals like you, me and us, to give up completely on the idea of a satisfying mortality. But no longer yeah?

I now know; who I am, what I am and what I can do, for I am now pain free

Divine or Higher Force

We all at some point need someone or something to pray to, no matter what race or creed we originate from. But the reality is when all said and done, we all as mortals are the only living beings able to solve complex mortal mysteries, so whilst it's okay I suspect to offer up prayers. I think it best that we all put our faith in ourselves and the endeavours of our fellow men.

My body is the greatest healer of them all and my mind is its engine

WEB SITES YOU MAY WISH TO EXPLORE

The information provided here is for research only; no responsibility will be accepted for the scope or content of any of these web sites.

1. www.doctormyhill.co.uk
2. www.biolab.co.uk/
3. www.thyroiduk.org/
4. www.nutramedix.com
5. www.mickeltherapy.com
6. www.moodcure.com/
7. www.reikifed.co.uk/
8. www.thyroidtears.co.uk/
9. www.paulocoelho.com/ *(My favourite Author)*

I now know; who I am, what I am and what I can do, for I am now pain free

OTHER BOOKS BY BARRY HARDY

Further personal insight and self help books written by Barry Hardy in relation to Raphael's Legacy include:

Raphael's Legacy
Stress at Close Quarters
Anxiety at Close Quarters
Exploring Fluid Normality
Arthritis at Close Quarters
Depression at Close Quarters
Fibromyalgia at Close Quarters
Lymes Disease at Close Quarters
Gulf War Syndrome at Close Quarters
Toxic Body Syndrome at Close Quarters
Myalgic Encephalopathy at Close Quarters
Chronic Fatigue Syndrome at Close Quarters
Bipolar / Manic Depression at Close Quarters
Obsessive Compulsive Disorder at Close Quarters

You can purchase any of these books at www.barryhardy.com

My body is the greatest healer of them all and my mind is its engine

DECENCY WARNING

This warning is repeated and placed at the back of this book because if you're like my daughter you're sure to start at the back of this book and I certainly don't wish to offend any back book readers either. Therefore please don't read this book if you are easily offended by:

- Strong views.
- Strong language.
- Grammatical inconsistencies and/or poor grammar.

Or

- Personal experiences and perceptions expressed freely.

I now know; who I am, what I am and what I can do, for I am now pain free

Personal Notes

My body is the greatest healer of them all and my mind is its engine

Personal Notes

I now know; who I am, what I am and what I can do, for I am now pain free

Personal Notes

My body is the greatest healer of them all and my mind is its engine

Personal Notes

I now know; who I am, what I am and what I can do, for I am now pain free

Personal Notes

My body is the greatest healer of them all and my mind is its engine

Personal Test Results

I now know; who I am, what I am and what I can do, for I am now pain free

Personal Test Results

My body is the greatest healer of them all and my mind is its engine

Personal Test Results

I now know; who I am, what I am and what I can do, for I am now pain free

Personal Test Results

My body is the greatest healer of them all and my mind is its engine

Personal Treatment Notes

I now know; who I am, what I am and what I can do, for I am now pain free

Personal Treatment Notes

My body is the greatest healer of them all and my mind is its engine

Personal Treatment Notes

I now know; who I am, what I am and what I can do, for I am now pain free

Personal Treatment Notes

My body is the greatest healer of them all and my mind is its engine

www.ingramcontent.com/pod-product-compliance
Ingram Content Group UK Ltd.
Pitfield, Milton Keynes, MK11 3LW, UK
UKHW041438180426
11947UKWH00007B/514